DEFENSE, SECURITY AND STRATEGIES

NAVY NUCLEAR-POWERED SURFACE SHIPS

DEFENSE, SECURITY AND STRATEGIES

Additional books in this series can be found on Nova's website under the Series tab.

Additional E-books in this series can be found on Nova's website under the E-books tab.

DEFENSE, SECURITY AND STRATEGIES

NAVY NUCLEAR-POWERED SURFACE SHIPS

RAUL CABITTA
AND
MARZIO ROCELLO
EDITORS

Nova Science Publishers, Inc.
New York

Copyright © 2011 by Nova Science Publishers, Inc.

All rights reserved. No part of this book may be reproduced, stored in a retrieval system or transmitted in any form or by any means: electronic, electrostatic, magnetic, tape, mechanical photocopying, recording or otherwise without the written permission of the Publisher.

For permission to use material from this book please contact us:
Telephone 631-231-7269; Fax 631-231-8175
Web Site: http://www.novapublishers.com

NOTICE TO THE READER
The Publisher has taken reasonable care in the preparation of this book, but makes no expressed or implied warranty of any kind and assumes no responsibility for any errors or omissions. No liability is assumed for incidental or consequential damages in connection with or arising out of information contained in this book. The Publisher shall not be liable for any special, consequential, or exemplary damages resulting, in whole or in part, from the readers' use of, or reliance upon, this material. Any parts of this book based on government reports are so indicated and copyright is claimed for those parts to the extent applicable to compilations of such works.

Independent verification should be sought for any data, advice or recommendations contained in this book. In addition, no responsibility is assumed by the publisher for any injury and/or damage to persons or property arising from any methods, products, instructions, ideas or otherwise contained in this publication.

This publication is designed to provide accurate and authoritative information with regard to the subject matter covered herein. It is sold with the clear understanding that the Publisher is not engaged in rendering legal or any other professional services. If legal or any other expert assistance is required, the services of a competent person should be sought. FROM A DECLARATION OF PARTICIPANTS JOINTLY ADOPTED BY A COMMITTEE OF THE AMERICAN BAR ASSOCIATION AND A COMMITTEE OF PUBLISHERS.

Additional color graphics may be available in the e-book version of this book.

Library of Congress Cataloging-in-Publication Data
Cabitta, Raul.
　Navy nuclear-powered surface ships / Raul Cabitta and Marzio Rocello.
　　p. cm.
　Includes index.
　ISBN 978-1-61470-790-5 (softcover)
　1. Nuclear warships--United States. 2. Nuclear warships--United States--Cost effectiveness. 3. Nuclear aircraft carriers--United States. I. Rocello, Marzio. II. Title.
　VA58.4.C32 2011
　623.825--dc23
　　　　　　　　　　　　2011026727

Published by Nova Science Publishers, Inc. † New York

CONTENTS

Preface		vii
Chapter 1	Navy Nuclear-Powered Surface Ships: Background, Issues, and Options for Congress *Ronald O'Rourke*	1
Chapter 2	The Cost-Effectiveness of Nuclear Power for Navy Surface Ships *Congress of the United States, Congressional Budget Office*	39
Chapter 3	Navy Ford (CVN-78) Class Aircraft Carrier Program: Background and Issues for Congress *Ronald O'Rourke*	73
Chapter Sources		101
Index		103

PREFACE

The U.S. Navy plans to build a number of new surface ships in the coming decades according to its most recent 30-year shipbuilding plan. All of the Navy's aircraft carriers are powered by nuclear reactors; its other surface combatants are powered by engines that use conventional petroleum-based fuels. The Navy could save money on fuel in the future by purchasing additional nuclear-powered ships rather than conventionally powered ships. Those savings in fuel costs, however, would be offset by the additional up-front costs required for the procurement of nuclear-powered ships. This book examines the cost-effectiveness of nuclear power for navy surface ships and the issues and options for Congress.

Chapter 1- All of the Navy's aircraft carriers, but none of its other surface ships, are nuclear-powered. Some Members of Congress, particularly on the House Armed Services Committee, have expressed interest in expanding the use of nuclear power to a wider array of Navy surface ships, starting with the CG(X), a planned new cruiser that the Navy had wanted to start procuring around FY2017. Section 1012 of the FY2008 Defense Authorization Act (H.R. 4986/P.L. 110-181 of January 28, 2008) made it U.S. policy to construct the major combatant ships of the Navy, including ships like the CG(X), with integrated nuclear power systems, unless the Secretary of Defense submits a notification to Congress that the inclusion of an integrated nuclear power system in a given class of ship is not in the national interest.

Chapter 2- The U.S. Navy plans to build a number of new surface ships in the coming decades, according to its most recent 30-year shipbuilding plan.[1] All of the Navy's aircraft carriers (and submarines) are powered by nuclear reactors; its other surface combatants are powered by engines that use conventional petroleum-based fuels. The Navy could save money on fuel in the future by purchasing additional nuclear-powered ships rather than conventionally powered ships. Those savings in fuel costs, however, would be offset by the additional up-front costs required for the procurement of nuclear-powered ships.

Chapter 3- CVN-78, CVN-79, and CVN-80 are the first three ships in the Navy's new Gerald R. Ford (CVN78) class of nuclear-powered aircraft carriers (CVNs).

CVN-78 was procured in FY2008 and is being funded with congressionally authorized four-year incremental funding in FY2008-FY2011. The Navy's proposed FY2012 budget estimates the ship's procurement cost at $11,531.0 million (i.e., about $11.5 billion) in then-year dollars. The Navy's proposed FY2011 budget requested $1,731.3 million in procurement funding as the final increment to complete this estimated procurement cost.

In: Navy Nuclear-Powered Surface Ships ISBN: 978-1-61470-790-5
Editors: R. Cabitta, M. Rocello © 2011 Nova Science Publishers, Inc.

Chapter 1

NAVY NUCLEAR-POWERED SURFACE SHIPS: BACKGROUND, ISSUES, AND OPTIONS FOR CONGRESS[*]

Ronald O'Rourke

SUMMARY

All of the Navy's aircraft carriers, but none of its other surface ships, are nuclear-powered. Some Members of Congress, particularly on the House Armed Services Committee, have expressed interest in expanding the use of nuclear power to a wider array of Navy surface ships, starting with the CG(X), a planned new cruiser that the Navy had wanted to start procuring around FY2017. Section 1012 of the FY2008 Defense Authorization Act (H.R. 4986/P.L. 110-181 of January 28, 2008) made it U.S. policy to construct the major combatant ships of the Navy, including ships like the CG(X), with integrated nuclear power systems, unless the Secretary of Defense submits a notification to Congress that the inclusion of an integrated nuclear power system in a given class of ship is not in the national interest.

The Navy studied nuclear power as a design option for the CG(X), but did not announce whether it would prefer to build the CG(X) as a nuclear-powered ship. The Navy's FY2011 budget proposed canceling

---

[*] This is an edited, reformatted and augmented version of a Congressional Research Service publication, CRS Report for Congress RL33946, from www.crs.gov, dated January 18, 2011.

the CG(X) program and instead building an improved version of the conventionally powered Arleigh Burke (DDG-51) class Aegis destroyer. The cancellation of the CG(X) program would appear to leave no near-term shipbuilding program opportunities for expanding the application of nuclear power to Navy surface ships other than aircraft carriers.

A 2006 Navy study on the potential for applying nuclear-power to Navy surface ships other than aircraft carriers concluded the following, among other things:

- In constant FY2007 dollars, building a Navy surface combatant or amphibious ship with nuclear power rather than conventional power would add roughly $600 million to $800 million to its procurement cost.
- The total life-cycle cost of a nuclear-powered medium-size surface combatant would equal that of a conventionally powered medium-size surface combatant if the cost of crude oil averages $70 per barrel to $225 per barrel over the life of the ship.
- Nuclear-power should be considered for near-term applications for medium-size surface combatants.
- Compared to conventionally powered ships, nuclear-powered ships have advantages in terms of both time needed to surge to a distant theater of operation for a contingency, and in terms of operational presence (time on station) in the theater of operation.

INTRODUCTION

All of the Navy's aircraft carriers, but none of its other surface ships, are nuclear-powered. Some Members of Congress, particularly on the House Armed Services Committee, have expressed interest in expanding the use of nuclear power to a wider array of Navy surface ships, starting with the CG(X), a planned new cruiser that the Navy had wanted to start procuring around FY2017. Section 1012 of the FY2008 Defense Authorization Act (H.R. 4986/P.L. 110-181 of January 28, 2008) made it U.S. policy to construct the major combatant ships of the Navy, including ships like the CG(X), with integrated nuclear power systems, unless the Secretary of Defense submits a notification to Congress that the inclusion of an integrated nuclear power system in a given class of ship is not in the national interest.

The Navy studied nuclear power as a design option for the CG(X), but did not announce whether it would prefer to build the CG(X) as a nuclear-powered ship. The Navy's FY2011 budget proposed canceling the CG(X) program and instead building an improved version of the conventionally powered Arleigh Burke (DDG-51) class Aegis destroyer.[1] The cancellation of the CG(X) program would appear to leave no near-term shipbuilding program opportunities for expanding the application of nuclear power to Navy surface ships other than aircraft carriers.

BACKGROUND

Nuclear and Conventional Power for Ships

Nuclear and Conventional Power in Brief

Most military ships and large commercial ships are conventionally powered, meaning that they burn a petroleum-based fuel, such as marine diesel, to generate power for propulsion and for operating shipboard equipment. Conventionally powered ships are sometimes called fossil fuel ships.

Some military ships are nuclear-powered, meaning that they use an on-board nuclear reactor to generate power for propulsion and shipboard equipment.[2] Nuclear-powered military ships are operated today by the United States, the United Kingdom, France, Russia, China, and India. Some other countries have expressed interest in, or conducted research and development work on, nuclear-powered military ships. A military ship's use of nuclear power is not an indication of whether it carries nuclear weapons—a nuclear-powered military ship can lack nuclear weapons, and a conventionally powered military ship can be armed with nuclear weapons.

Nuclear Power for a Surface Combatant

For a surface combatant like a cruiser, using nuclear power rather than conventional power eliminates the need for the ship to periodically refuel during extended operations at sea. Refueling a ship during a long-distance transit can reduce its average transit speed. Refueling a ship that is located in a theater of operations can temporarily reduce its ability to perform its missions. A nuclear-powered surface combatant can steam at sustained high speeds to a distant theater of operations, commence operations in the theater immediately upon arrival, and continue operating in the theater over time, all without a need for refueling.[3]

In contrast, a conventionally powered surface combatant might need to slow down for at-sea refueling at least once during a high-speed, long-distance transit; might need to refuel again upon arriving at the theater of operations; and might need to refuel periodically while in the theater of operations, particularly if the ship's operations in theater require frequent or continuous movement.

Table 1 shows the unrefueled cruising ranges of the Navy's existing conventionally powered cruisers and destroyers at a speed of 20 knots, along with transit distances from major U.S. Navy home ports to potential U.S. Navy operating areas. Navy surface combatants have maximum sustained speeds of more than 30 knots. A speed of 20 knots is a moderately fast long-distance transit speed for a Navy surface combatant. For a higher transit speed, such as 25 knots, the unrefueled cruising ranges would be less than those shown in the table, because the amount of fuel needed to travel a certain distance rises with ship speed, particularly as speeds increase above about 15 knots.

Table 1. Unrefueled Cruising Ranges and Transit Distances (in nautical miles)

Unrefueled cruising ranges at 20 knots	
Arleigh Burke (DDG-51) class destroyer	4,400
Ticonderoga (CG-47) class cruiser	6,000
Transit distances	
Pearl Harbor, HI, to area east of Taiwan[a,b]	4,283
San Diego, CA, to area east of Taiwan[a,c]	5,933
Pearl Harbor, HI, to Persian Gulf (via Singapore)	~9,500
San Diego, CA, to Persian Gulf (via Singapore)[c]	~11,300
Norfolk to Persian Gulf (via Suez canal)	~8,300

Sources: For ship unrefueled cruising ranges: Norman Polmar, *The Naval Institute Guide to the Ships and Aircraft of the U.S. Fleet*, 18th ed., Annapolis (MD), 2005. For transit distances to area east of Taiwan: Straight line distances calculated by the "how far is it" calculator, available at http://www.indo.com/distance/. (Actual transit distances may be greater due to the possible need for ships to depart from a straight-line course so as to avoid land barriers, remain within port-area shipping channels, etc.) For transit distances to Persian Gulf: Defense Mapping Agency, *Distances Between Ports* (Pub. 151), 7th ed., 1993, with distances shown for reaching a position roughly in the center of the Persian Gulf.

[a] Area east of Taiwan defined as a position in the sea at 24°N, 124°E, which is roughly 130 nautical miles east of Taiwan.

[b] Distance from Pearl Harbor calculated from Honolulu, which is about 6 nautical miles southeast of Pearl Harbor.

[c] For transit distances from the Navy home port at Everett, WA, north of Seattle, rather than from San Diego, subtract about 700 nm.

During extended operations at sea, a nuclear-powered surface combatant, like a conventionally powered one, might need to be resupplied with food, weapons (if sufficient numbers are expended in combat), and other supplies. These resupply operations can temporarily reduce the ship's ability to perform its missions.

U.S. Navy Nuclear-Powered Ships

Naval Nuclear Propulsion Program

The Navy's nuclear propulsion program began in 1948. The Navy's first nuclear-powered ship, the submarine Nautilus (SSN-571), was commissioned into service on September 30, 1954, and went to sea for the first time on January 17, 1955. The Navy's first nuclear-powered surface ships, the cruiser Long Beach (CGN-9) and the aircraft carrier Enterprise (CVN-65), were commissioned into service on September 9, 1961, and November 25, 1961, respectively.

The Navy's nuclear propulsion program is overseen and directed by an office called Naval Reactors (NR), which exists simultaneously as a part of both the Navy (where it forms a part of the Naval Sea Systems Command) and the Department of Energy (where it forms a part of the National Nuclear Security Administration). NR has broad, cradle-to-grave responsibility for the Navy's nuclear-propulsion program. This responsibility is set forth in Executive Order 12344 of February 1, 1982, the text of which was effectively incorporated into the U.S. Code (at 50 USC 2511)[4] by Section 1634 of the FY1985 defense authorization act (H.R. 5167/P.L. 98-525 of October 19, 1984) and again by section 3216 of the FY2000 defense authorization act (S. 1059/P.L. 106-65 of October 5, 1999). NR has established a reputation for maintaining very high safety standards for engineering and operating Navy nuclear power plants.

The first director of NR was Admiral Hyman Rickover, who served in the position from 1948 until 1982. Rickover is sometimes referred to as the father of the nuclear Navy. The current director is Admiral Kirkland Donald, who became director in November 2004. He is the fifth person to hold the position.

Current Navy Nuclear-Powered Ships

All of the Navy's submarines and all of its aircraft carriers are nuclear-powered. No other Navy ships are currently nuclear-powered. The Navy's combat submarine force has been entirely nuclear-powered since 1990.[5] The

Navy's aircraft carrier force became entirely nuclear-powered on May 12, 2009, with the retirement of the Kitty Hawk (CV-63), the Navy's last remaining conventionally powered carrier.

Earlier Navy Nuclear-Powered Cruisers

Although no Navy surface ships other than aircraft carriers are currently nuclear-powered, the Navy in the past built and operated nine nuclear-powered cruisers (CGNs). The nine ships, which are shown in Table 2, include three one-of-a-kind designs (CGNs 9, 25, and 35) followed by the two-ship California (CGN-36) class and the four-ship Virginia (CGN-38) class. All nine ships were decommissioned in the 1990s.

The nuclear-powered cruisers shown in Table 2 were procured to provide nuclear-powered escorts for the Navy's nuclear-powered carriers. Procurement of nuclear-powered cruisers was halted after FY1975 largely due to a desire to constrain the procurement costs of future cruisers. In deciding in the late 1970s on the design for the new cruiser that would carry the Aegis defense system, two nuclear-powered Aegis-equipped options—a 17,200-ton nuclear-powered strike cruiser (CSGN) and a 12,100-ton derivative of the CGN-38 class design—were rejected in favor of a third option of placing the Aegis system onto the smaller, conventionally powered hull originally developed for the Spruance (DD-963) class destroyer. The CSGN was estimated to have a procurement cost twice that of the DD-963-based option, while the CGN-42 was estimated to have a procurement cost 30%-50% greater than that of the DD-963-based option. The DD-963- based option became the 9,500-ton Ticonderoga (CG-47) class Aegis cruiser. The first Aegis cruiser was procured in FY1978.

Initial Fuel Core Included in Procurement Cost

The initial fuel core for a Navy nuclear-powered ship is installed during the construction of the ship. The procurement cost of the fuel core is included in the total procurement cost of the ship, which is funded in the Navy's shipbuilding budget, known formally as the Shipbuilding and Conversion, Navy (SCN) appropriation account. In constant FY2007 dollars, the initial fuel core for a Virginia (SSN-774) class submarine cost about $170 million, and the initial fuel cores for an aircraft carrier (which uses two reactors and therefore has two fuel cores) had a combined cost of about $660 million.[6]

The procurement cost of a conventionally powered Navy ship, in contrast, does not include the cost of petroleum-based fuel needed to operate the ship, and this fuel is procured largely through the Operation and Maintenance, Navy (OMN) appropriation account.

Table 2. Earlier Navy Nuclear-Powered Cruisers

Hull number	Name	Builder	Displacement (tons)	Procured	Entered service	Decommissioned
CGN-9	Long Beach	Bethlehem[a]	17,100	FY57	1961	1995
CGN-25	Bainbridge	Bethlehem[a]	8,580	FY59	1962	1996
CGN-35	Truxtun	New York[b]	8,800	FY62	1967	1995
CGN-36	California	NGSB[c]	10,530	FY67	1974	1999
CGN-37	South Carolina	NGSB[c]	10,530	FY68	1975	1999
CGN-38	Virginia	NGSB[c]	11,300	FY70	1976	1994
CGN-39	Texas	NGSB[c]	11,300	FY71	1977	1993
CGN-40	Mississippi	NGSB[c]	11,300	FY72	1978	1997
CGN-41	Arkansas	NGSB[c]	11,300	FY75	1980	1998

Source: Prepared by CRS based on Navy data and Norman Polmar, *The Ships and Aircraft of the U.S. Fleet.*

[a] Bethlehem Steel, Quincy, MA.

[b] New York Shipbuilding, Camden, NJ.

[c] Newport News Shipbuilding, which forms a part of Northrop Grumman Shipbuilding (NGSB).

Section 1012 of FY2008 Defense Authorization Act (P.L. 110-181)

Section 1012 of the FY2008 Defense Authorization Act (H.R. 4986/P.L. 110-181 of January 28, 2008) made it U.S. policy to construct the major combatant ships of the Navy, including ships like the CG(X), with integrated nuclear power systems, unless the Secretary of Defense submits a notification to Congress that the inclusion of an integrated nuclear power system in a given class of ship is not in the national interest.

The FY2010 defense authorization bill (S. 1390) as reported by the Senate Armed Services Committee (S.Rept. 111-35 of July 2, 2009) contained a provision (Section 1012) that would repeal Section 1012 of the FY2008 defense authorization act. The House Armed Services Committee, in its report (H.Rept. 111-166 of June 18, 2009) on the FY2010 defense authorization bill (H.R. 2647), stated that it "remains committed to the direction" of Section 1012 of the FY2008 defense authorization act. The conference report (H.Rept.

111-288 of October 7, 2009) on the FY2010 defense authorization act (H.R. 2647/P.L. 111-84 of October 28, 2009) did not contain a provision repealing or amending Section 1012 of the FY2008 defense authorization act.

CG(X) Cruiser Program[7]

The Program in General

The CG(X) cruiser was a planned replacement for the Navy's 22 Aegis cruisers, which are projected to reach retirement age between 2021 and 2029. The Navy originally wanted to build as many as 19 CG(X)s, with the first to be procured around FY2017.[8]

The Navy assessed CG(X) design options in a large study called the CG(X) Analysis of Alternatives (AOA), known more formally as the Maritime Air and Missile Defense of Joint Forces (MAMDJF) AOA. The Navy did not announce whether it would prefer to build the CG(X) as a nuclear-powered ship. The Navy stated that it wanted to equip the CG(X) with a combat system featuring a powerful radar capable of supporting ballistic missile defense (BMD) operations.[9] The Navy testified that this combat system was to have a power output of 30 or 31 megawatts, which is several times the power output of the combat system on the Navy's existing cruisers and destroyers.[10] This suggested that in terms of power used for combat system operations, the CG(X) might have used substantially more energy over the course of its life than the Navy's existing cruisers and destroyers. As discussed later in this report, a ship's life-cycle energy use is a factor in evaluating the economic competitiveness of nuclear power compared to conventional power.

Reactor Plant for a Nuclear-Powered CG(X)

The Navy testified in 2007 that in the Navy's 2006 study on alternative ship propulsion systems (see "2006 Navy Alternative Propulsion Study" below), the notional medium-sized surface combatant in the study (which the study defined as a ship with a displacement between 21,000 metric tons and 26,000 metric tons) used a modified version of one-half of the reactor plant that the Navy has developed for its new Gerald R. Ford (CVN-78) class aircraft carriers, also called the CVN-21 class.[11] The Ford-class reactor plant, like the reactor plant on the Navy's existing Nimitz (CVN-68) class aircraft carriers, is a twin reactor plant that includes two nuclear reactors.[12] The medium-sized surface combatant employed a modified version of one-half of this plant, with a single reactor.

This suggested that if the CG(X) were a ship with a displacement of 21,000 or more metric tons, its reactor plant could have been a modified version of one-half of the Ford-class reactor plant. This approach would minimize the time and cost of developing a reactor plant for a nuclear-powered CG(X). In the Ford class, the initial nuclear fuel cores in the two reactors are to be sufficient to power the ship for one-half of its expected life of 40 to 50 years. In a nuclear-powered CG(X), the Navy said, the initial fuel core in the single reactor would be sufficient to power the ship for its entire expected life of 30 to 35 years. Since the two fuel cores for an aircraft carrier cost about $660 million in constant FY2007 dollars (see previous section on initial fuel cores), the cost of a single fuel core for a CG(X) might be about $330 million in constant FY2007 dollars.

Proposed Cancellation of Program
The Navy's FY2011 budget proposed canceling the CG(X) program and instead building an improved version of the conventionally powered Arleigh Burke (DDG-51) class Aegis destroyer.[13] The cancellation of the CG(X) program would appear to leave no near-term shipbuilding program opportunities for expanding the application of nuclear power to Navy surface ships other than aircraft carriers.

Construction Shipyards

Nuclear-Capable Shipyards
Two U.S. shipyards are currently certified to build nuclear-powered ships—Newport news Shipbuilding of Newport News, VA, which forms part of Northrop Grumman Shipbuilding (NGSB); and General Dynamics' Electric Boat Division (GD/EB) of Groton, CT, and Quonset Point, RI. Newport News can build nuclear-powered surface ships and nuclear-powered submarines. GD/EB can build nuclear-powered submarines. Newport News built all the Navy's nuclear-powered aircraft carriers. Newport News also built the final six nuclear-powered cruisers shown in Table 2. Newport News and GD/EB together have built every Navy nuclear-powered submarine procured since FY1969.

Although Newport News and GD/EB are the only U.S. shipyards that currently build nuclear-powered ships for the Navy, five other U.S. shipyards once did so as well.[14] These five yards built 44 of the 107 nuclear-powered submarines that were procured for the Navy through FY1968. Two of these five yards built the first three nuclear-powered cruisers shown in Table 2.

Surface Combatant Shipyards
All cruisers and destroyers procured for the Navy since FY1978 have been built at two shipyards—General Dynamics' Bath Iron Works (GD/BIW) of Bath, ME, and the Ingalls shipyard at Pascagoula, MS, that forms part of NGSB. GD/BIW has never built nuclear-powered ships. Ingalls is one of the five U.S. yards other than Newport News and GD/EB that once built nuclear-powered ships. Ingalls built 12 nuclear-powered submarines, the last being the Parche (SSN-683), which was procured in FY1968, entered service in 1974, and retired in 2005.[15] Ingalls also overhauled or refueled 11 nuclear-powered submarines. Ingalls' nuclear facility was decommissioned in 1980, and Ingalls is not certified to build nuclear-powered ships.[16]

Recent Navy Studies for Congress

The Navy in recent years has conducted two studies for Congress on the potential cost-effectiveness of expanding the use of nuclear power to a wider array of surface ships. These studies are the 2005 Naval Reactors quick look analysis, and the more comprehensive and detailed 2006 Navy alternative propulsion study. Each of these is discussed below.

2005 Naval Reactors Quick Look Analysis
The 2005 NR quick look analysis was conducted at the request of Representative Roscoe Bartlett, who was then chairman of the Projection Forces Subcommittee of the House Armed Services Committee (since renamed the Seapower and Expeditionary Forces Subcommittee). The analysis concluded that the total life-cycle cost (meaning the sum of procurement cost, life-cycle operating and support cost, and post-retirement disposal cost) of a nuclear-powered version of a large-deck (LHA-type) amphibious assault ship would equal that of a conventionally powered version of such a ship if the cost of crude oil over the life of the ship averaged about $70 per barrel. The study concluded that the total life-cycle cost of a nuclear-powered surface combatant would equal that of a conventionally powered version if the cost of crude oil over the life of the ship averaged about $178 per barrel. This kind of calculation is called a life-cycle cost break-even analysis. The study noted but

did not attempt to quantify the mobility-related operational advantages of nuclear propulsion for a surface ship.[17]

2006 Navy Alternative Propulsion Study

The more comprehensive and detailed 2006 Navy alternative propulsion study was conducted in response to Section 130 of the FY2006 defense authorization act (H.R. 1815, P.L. 109-163 of January 6, 2006), which called for such a study (see "Prior-Year Legislative Activity"). The study reached a number of conclusions, including the following:

- In constant FY2007 dollars, building a Navy surface combatant or amphibious ship with nuclear power rather than conventional power would add roughly $600 million to $800 million to its procurement cost.
    — For a small surface combatant, the procurement-cost increase was about $600 million.
    — For a medium-size combatant (defined as a ship with a displacement between 21,000 metric tons and 26,000 metric tons), the increase was about $600 million to about $700 million.
    — For an amphibious ship, the increase was about $800 million.[18]
- Although nuclear-powered ships have higher procurement costs than conventionally powered ships, they have lower operating and support costs when fuel costs are taken into account.
- A ship's operational tempo and resulting level of energy use significantly influences the life-cycle cost break-even analysis. The higher the operational tempo and resulting level of energy use assumed for the ship, lower the cost of crude oil needed to break even on a life-cycle cost basis, and the more competitive nuclear power becomes in terms of total life-cycle cost.
- The newly calculated life-cycle cost break-even cost-ranges, which supercede the break-even cost figures from the 2005 NR quick look analysis, are as follows:
    —$210 per barrel to $670 per barrel for a small surface combatant;
    —$70 per barrel to $225 per barrel for a medium-size surface combatant; and
    —$210 per barrel to $290 per barrel for an amphibious ship. In each case, the lower dollar figure is for a high ship operating

- tempo, and the higher dollar figure is for a low ship operating tempo.
- At a crude oil cost of $74.15 per barrel (which was a market price at certain points in 2006), the life-cycle cost premium of nuclear power is:
    —17% to 37% for a small surface combatant;
    —0% to 10% for a medium sized surface combatant; and —7% to 8% for an amphibious ship.
- The life-cycle cost break-even analysis indicates that nuclear-power should be considered for near-term applications for medium-size surface combatants, and that life-cycle cost will not drive the selection of nuclear power for small surface combatants or amphibious ships. A nuclear-powered medium-size surface combatant is the most likely of the three ship types studied to prove economical, depending on the operating tempo that the ship actually experiences over its lifetime.
- Compared to conventionally powered ships, nuclear-powered ships have advantages in terms of both time needed to surge to a distant theater of operation for a contingency, and operational presence (time on station) in the theater of operation.[19]

POTENTIAL ISSUES FOR CONGRESS

No Apparent Near-Term Shipbuilding Program Opportunities

The cancellation of the CG(X) program would appear to leave no near-term shipbuilding program opportunities for expanding the application of nuclear power to Navy surface ships other than aircraft carriers.

Assessing Whether Any Future Ship Classes Should Be Nuclear Powered

In assessing whether any future classes of Navy surface ships (in addition to aircraft carriers) should be nuclear-powered, Congress may consider a number of issues, including cost, operational effectiveness, ship construction, ship maintenance and repair, crew training, ports calls and forward homeporting, and environmental impact. Each of these is discussed below.

Cost

Development and Design Cost

The cost calculations presented in the 2006 Navy alternative propulsion study do not include the additional up-front design and development costs, if any, for a nuclear-powered surface ship. As discussed in the "Background" section, if the CG(X) were to displace 21,000 or more metric tons, the Navy could have the option of fitting the CG(X) with a modified version of one-half of the Ford (CVN-78) class aircraft carrier nuclear power plant. This could minimize the up-front development cost of the CG(X) nuclear power plant. If the CG(X) were not large enough to accommodate a modified version of one-half of the Ford-class plant, then a new nuclear plant would need to be designed for the CG(X). Although this new plant could use components common to the Ford-class plant or other existing Navy nuclear plants, the cost of developing this new plant would likely be greater than the cost of modifying the Ford-class plant design.

Procurement Cost

For the CG(X)

The Navy originally stated a preference for basing the design of the CG(X) on the design of its new Zumwalt (DDG-1000) class destroyer, which is a conventionally powered ship. This approach could result in a conventionally powered CG(X) design with a procurement cost similar to that of the DDG-1000. If a conventionally powered CG(X) were to have a procurement cost equal to that of the DDG-1000 design, then a nuclear-powered CG(X) might cost roughly 32% to 37% more than a conventionally powered CG(X).[20] If a conventionally powered CG(X) were to have a procurement cost greater than that of the DDG-1000, then the percentage procurement cost premium for nuclear power for the CG(X) would be less than 32% to 37%. The 2006 Navy study states that for a medium-size surface combatant that is larger than the DDG-1000, an additional cost of about $600 million to $700 million would equate to a procurement cost increase of about 22%. In more recent years, however, the Navy appeared to back away from the idea of basing the design of the CG(X) on the design of the DDG-1000.

If building a Navy surface combatant or amphibious ship with nuclear power rather than conventional power would add roughly $600 million to $700 million to its procurement cost, then procuring one or two nuclear-powered CG(X)s per year, as called for in the Navy's 30-year shipbuilding plan, would cost roughly $600 million to $1,400 million more per year than procuring one or two conventionally powered CG(X)s per year, and procuring a force of 19 nuclear-powered CG(X)s would cost roughly $11.4 billion to $13.3 billion more than procuring a force of 19 conventionally powered CG(X)s. A figure of $13.3 is comparable to the total amount of funding in the Navy's shipbuilding budget in certain recent years.

For Submarines and Aircraft Carriers

The Navy in 2007 estimated that building the CG(X) or other future Navy surface ships with nuclear power could reduce the production cost of nuclear-propulsion components for submarines and aircraft carriers by 5% to 9%, depending on the number of nuclear-powered surface ships that are built.[21] Building one nuclear-powered cruiser every two years, the Navy has testified, might reduce nuclear-propulsion component costs by about 7%. In a steady-state production environment, the Navy testified in 2007, the savings might equate to about $115 million for each aircraft carrier, and about $35 million for each submarine.

The Navy stated that this "is probably the most optimistic estimate."[22] The Navy states that these savings were not included in the cost calculations presented in the 2006 Navy study.

BWXT, a principal maker of nuclear-propulsion components for Navy ships, estimated in 2007 that increasing Virginia-class submarine procurement from one boat per year to two boats per year would reduce the cost of nuclear propulsion components 9% for submarines and 8% for aircraft carriers, and that "Adding a nuclear[-powered] cruiser or [nuclear-powered] large-deck amphibious ship would significantly drive down nuclear power plant costs across the fleet, even beyond the savings associated with the second Virginia-class [submarine per year]."[23]

Total Life-Cycle Cost

As suggested by the 2006 Navy study, the total-life-cycle cost break-even analysis can be affected by projections of future oil prices and ship operating tempo.

Future Oil Prices

Views on potential future oil prices vary.[24] Some supporters of using nuclear power for the CG(X) and other future Navy surface ships, such as Representative Roscoe Bartlett, a member of the House Armed Services Committee, believe that oil in coming decades may become increasingly expensive, or that guaranteed access to oil may become more problematic, and that this is a central reason for making the CG(X) or other future Navy surface ships nuclearpowered.[25]

Ship Operating Tempo
A ship's average lifetime operating tempo can be affected by the number of wars, crises, and other contingency operations that it participates in over its lifetime, because such events can involve operating tempos that are higher than those of "normal" day-to-day operations. Ship operating tempo can also be affected by the size of the Navy. The lower the number of ships in the Navy, for example, the higher the operating tempo each a ship might be required to sustain for the fleet to accomplish a given set of missions.

CG(X) vs. Medium-Size Surface Combatant
If the CG(X) were based on the hull design of the 14,500-ton DDG-1000 destroyer, the CG(X) may be smaller the 21,000- to 26,000-ton medium-size surface combatant in the 2006 Navy study. What difference that might create between the CG(X) and the medium-size surface combatant in terms of life-cycle energy use, and thus life-cycle cost break-even range, is not clear. The Navy has testified that the medium sized surface combatant in the 2006 study was modeled with a radar requiring 30 or 31 megawatts of power, like the radar the Navy wants to install on the CG(X).[26]

Operational Effectiveness

Operational Value of Increased Ship Mobility
What is the operational value of increased ship mobility? How much better can a ship perform its missions as a result of this increased mobility? And is there some way to translate the mobility advantages of nuclear power into dollar terms? One potential way to translate the value of increased ship mobility into dollar terms would be to determine how much aggregate capability a force of 19 conventionally powered CG(X)s would have for surging to distant theaters and for maintaining on-station presence in theater, then determine how many nuclear-powered CG(X)s would be required to provide the same aggregate capability, and then compare the total cost of the 19 conventionally powered CG(X)s to the total cost of the nuclear-powered CG(X) force.

Potential Other Operational Advantages of Nuclear Power

Are there operational advantages of nuclear power for a surface ship other than increased ship mobility? One possibility concerns ship detectability. A nuclear-powered ship does not require an exhaust stack as part of its deckhouse, and does not emit hot exhaust gases. Other things held equal, this might make a nuclear-powered surface ship less detectable than a conventionally powered ship, particularly to infrared sensors. This possible advantage for the nuclear-powered ship might be either offset or reinforced by possible differences between the nuclear-powered ship and the conventionally powered ship in other areas, such as the temperature of the engine compartment (which again might affect infrared detectability) or the level of machinery noise (which might affect acoustic detectability).

Some supporters of building future Navy surface ships with nuclear power have argued that an additional operational advantage of nuclear power for surface ships would be to reduce the Navy's dependence on its relatively small force of refueling oilers, and thus the potential impact on fleet operations of an enemy attack on those oilers. The Navy acknowledges that potential attacks on oilers are a concern, but argues that the fleet's vulnerability to such attacks is recognized and that oilers consequently are treated as high-value ships in terms of measures taken to protect them from attack.[27]

Another potential advantage of nuclear power postulated by some observers is that a nuclear-powered ship can use its reactor to provide electrical power for use ashore for extended periods of time, particularly to help localities that are experiencing brownouts during peak use periods or whose access to electrical power from the grid has been disrupted by a significant natural disaster or terrorist attack. The Navy stated that the CG(X) was to have a total power-generating capacity of about 80 megawatts (MW). Some portion of that would be needed to operate the reactor plant itself and other essential equipment aboard the ship. Much of the rest might be available for transfer off the ship. For purposes of comparison, a typical U.S. commercial power plant might have a capacity of 300 MW to 1000 MW. A single megawatt can be enough to meet the needs of several hundred U.S. homes, depending on the region of the country and other factors.[28]

Skeptics of the idea of using nuclear-powered ships to generate electrical power for use ashore could argue that if the local transmission system has been disrupted, the ship's generation capacity may be of limited use in restoring electric power. If the local transmission system is intact, they could argue, onshore infrastructure would be required to transmit the ship's power into the local system. The military or a local utility, they could argue, would likely bear the cost for this infrastructure, which would be used only on a sporadic basis. Skeptics could argue that a Navy ship would be helpful only if the power emergency lasts longer than the time it would take for the ship to reach the connection point. If the nearest available Navy ship is several steaming days away from the connection point when the power emergency occurs, they could argue, the ship might not be able arrive before local power is partially or fully restored. Skeptics could argue that critical facilities in the area of the power emergency, such as hospitals, would likely be equipped with emergency back-up diesel generators to respond to short-term loss of power.[29]

Ship Construction

Shipyards

Another potential issue for Congress to consider in weighing whether future Navy surface ships (in addition to aircraft carriers) should be nuclear-powered concerns the shipyards that would be used to build the ships. There are at least three potential approaches for building a nuclear-powered version of a major surface combatant like the CG(X):

- Build them at Newport News, with GD/EB possibly contributing to the construction of the ships' nuclear portions.
- Certify Ingalls and/or GD/BIW to build nuclear-powered ships, and then build the CG(X)s at those yards.
- Build the nuclear portions of the CG(X)s at Newport News and/or GD/EB, the non-nuclear portions at Ingalls and/or GD/BIW, and perform final assembly, integration, and test work for the ships at either
  —Newport News and/or GD/EB, or
  —Ingalls and/or GD/BIW.

These options have significant potential implications for workloads and employment levels at each of these shipyards.

On the question of what would be needed to certify Ingalls and/or GD/BIW to build nuclear-powered ships, the director of NR testified that:

> Just the basics of what it takes to have a nuclear-certified yard, to build one from scratch, or even if one existed once upon a time as it did at Pasacagoula, and we shut it down, first and foremost you have to have the facilities to do that. What that includes, and I have just some notes here, but such things as you have to have the docks and the dry-docks and the pier capability to support nuclear ships, whatever that would entail. You

would have to have lifting and handling equipment, cranes, that type of thing; construction facilities to build the special nuclear components, and to store those components and protect them in the way that would be required.

The construction facilities would be necessary for handling fuel and doing the fueling operations that would be necessary on the ship—those types of things. And then the second piece is, and probably the harder piece other than just kind of the brick-and-mortar type, is building the structures, the organizations in place to do that work, for instance, nuclear testing, specialized nuclear engineering, nuclear production work. If you look, for instance, at Northrop Grumman Newport News, right now, just to give you a perspective of the people you are talking about in those departments, it is on the order of 769 people in nuclear engineering; 308 people in the major lines of control department; 225 in nuclear quality assurance; and then almost 2,500 people who do nuclear production work. So all of those would have to be, you would have to find that workforce, certify and qualify them, to be able to do that.[30]

The director of NR testified that Newport News and GD/BIW "have sufficient capacity to accommodate nuclear-powered surface ship construction, and therefore there is no need to make the substantial investment in time and dollars necessary to generate additional excess capacity."[31] In light of this, the Navy testified, only the first and third options above are "viable."[32] The director of NR testified that:

> my view of this is we have some additional capacity at both Electric Boat and at Northrop Grumman Newport News. My primary concern is if we are serious about building another nuclear-powered warship, a new class of warship, cost is obviously going to be some degree of concern, and certainly this additional costs, which would be—and I don't have a number to give you right now, but I think you can see it would be substantial to do it even if you could. It probably doesn't help our case to move down the path toward building another nuclear-powered case, when we have the capability existing already in those existing yards.[33]

With regard to the third option of building the nuclear portions of the ships at Newport News and/or GD/EB, and the non-nuclear portions at Ingalls and/or GD/BIW, the Navy testified that the "Location of final ship erection would require additional analysis." One Navy official, however, expressed a potential preference for performing final assembly, integration, and test work at Newport News or GD/EB, stating that:

we are building warships in modular sections now. So if we were going to [ask], "Could you assemble this [ship], could you build modules of this ship in different yards and put it together in a nuclear-certified yard?", the answer is yes, definitely, and we do that today with the Virginia Class [submarine program]. As you know, we are barging modules of [that type of] submarine up and down the coast.

What I would want is, and sort of following along with what [NR director] Admiral [Kirkland] Donald said, you would want the delivering yard to be the yard where the reactor plant was built, tooled, and tested, because they have the expertise to run through all of that nuclear work and test and certify the ship and take it out on sea trials.

But the modules of the non-reactor plant, which is the rest of the ship, could be built theoretically at other yards and barged or transported in other fashion to the delivering shipyard. If I had to do it ideally, that is where I would probably start talking to my industry partners, because although we have six [large] shipyards [for building large navy ships], it is really two corporations [that own them], and those two corporations each own what is now a surface combatant shipyard and they each own a nuclear-capable shipyard. I would say if we were going to go do this, we would sit down with them and say, you know, from a corporation standpoint, what would be the best work flow? What would be the best place to construct modules? And how would you do the final assembly and testing of a nuclear-powered warship?[34]

Nuclear-Propulsion Component Manufacturers

A related issue that Congress may consider in weighing whether future Navy surface ships (in addition to aircraft carriers) should be nuclear-powered is whether there is sufficient capacity at the firms that make nuclear-propulsion components to accommodate the increase in production volume that would result from building such ships with nuclear power. On this question, the Navy has testified:

> Right now, as I look across the industrial base that provides [for nuclear-powered ships], let's just talk about the components, for instance, and I just look across that base, because we have been asserting earlier that we were going to go to [a procurement rate of two Virginia-class submarines per year] earlier [than the currently planned year of FY2012], we had facilitized and have sustained an over-capacity in those facilities to support construction of those additional components. So right now, it depends on the vendor and which one is doing what, the capacity is running right now at probably about 65 percent of what it could be doing, on the order of that. Again, it varies depending on the vendor specifically.

So there is additional capacity in there, and even with the addition of a second Virginia-class submarine, there is still a margin in there, if you are talking about a single cruiser in the early phases of design, we still have margin in there that I believe we can sustain that work in addition to the submarine work within the industrial base.

We would have to look at that in more detail once we determine what the design looks like and the degree to which we can use existing components. If you had to design new components, that would add a little bit more complexity to it, but that is a rough estimate of what I would provide for you now.[35]

Ship Maintenance and Repair

Building future Navy surface ships (in addition to aircraft carriers) with nuclear power could affect the future distribution of Navy ship maintenance and repair work, because only certain U.S. shipyards are qualified for performing certain kinds of work on nuclear-powered ships. Much of the maintenance and repair work done on nuclear-powered ships is done at the country's four government-operated naval shipyards (NSYs)—Portsmouth NSY at Kittery, ME, Norfolk NSY at Norfolk, VA; Puget Sound NSY at Bremerton, WA; and Pearl Harbor NSY at Pearl Harbor, HI. Newport News and GD/EB also perform some maintenance and repair work on nuclear-powered ships.

Crew Training

Would the Navy have the capacity to train the additional nuclear-qualified sailors that would be needed to crew additional nuclear-powered ships? On this question, the director of NR testified that "My training pipeline does have the capacity without further infrastructure investment to produce the additional personnel required by future classes of [nuclear-powered] ships." He also stated:

> We, in looking at the training pipeline, there are a couple of dynamics that are in work right now. First off, the [nuclear-powered aircraft carrier] Enterprise is going to be going away [in 2013], and that is a pretty significant training load just to keep that crew operating.[36] And also, there as the CVN-21 [carrier class] comes on, [that is, as] the Ford-class carriers come on, and the [Nimitz-class nuclear-powered carriers] start to go away, [the number of people required to crew carriers will decrease, because with the] Ford class, we are targeting a 50 percent reduction in the reactor department sizing over there [compared to the Nimitz class].

So for the foreseeable future, the training infrastructure that we have right now will meet the needs to sustain this [additional] class [of nuclear-powered ship], if you choose to do it.[37]

Port Calls and Forward Homeporting

A nuclear-powered ship might be less welcome than a conventionally powered ship in the ports of countries with strong anti-nuclear sentiments. The Navy works to minimize this issue in connection with its nuclear-powered submarines and aircraft carriers, and states that "U.S. nuclear-powered warships are welcome today in over 150 ports in more than 50 countries worldwide, thus allowing our warships to carry out their mission without constraint."[38]

Some Navy ships are forward-homeported, meaning that they are homeported in foreign countries that are close to potential U.S. Navy operating areas overseas. Forward-homeported Navy ships have occasional need for access to maintenance facilities near their home ports, and foreign shipyards are not qualified to perform certain kinds of maintenance work on nuclear-powered Navy ships. Building Navy surface ships (in addition to aircraft carriers) with nuclear power might thus affect the number of potentially suitable locations for forward-homeporting the ships, should the Navy decide that forward homeporting them would be desirable for purposes of shortening transit times to and from potential operating areas.

Environmental Impact

Conventionally powered ships exhaust greenhouse gases and other pollutants that are created through combustion of petroleum-based fuel. They can also leak fuel into the water, particularly if they are damaged in an accident (such as a collision) or by enemy attack. Other environmental impacts of conventionally powered ships include those associated with extracting oil from the ground, transporting it to a refinery, refining it into fuel, and transporting that fuel to the ship. Most of these activities produce additional greenhouse gases and other pollutants.

Nuclear-powered ships do not exhaust greenhouse gases and other pollutants created through conventional combustion. The environmental impacts of nuclear-powered ships include those associated with mining and processing uranium to fuel reactors, and with storing and disposing of spent nuclear fuel cores, radioactive waste water from reactors, and the reactors and other radioactive components of retired nuclear-powered ships. As mentioned in the "Background" section, NR has established a reputation for maintaining very high safety standards for engineering and operating Navy nuclear power plants. In addition, Navy combat ships are built to withstand significant shock and battle damage. It is possible, however, that a very serious accident involving a nuclear-powered Navy ship (such as a major collision) or a major enemy attack on a nuclear-powered Navy ship might damage the ship's hull and reactor compartment enough to cause a release of radioactivity, which may have adverse effects on the environment.

LEGISLATIVE ACTIVITY FOR FY2011

FY2011 Defense Authorization Act (H.R. 6523/P.L. 111-383)

House (H.R. 5136)
The House Armed Services Committee, in its report (H.Rept. 111-491 of May 21, 2010) on the FY2011 defense authorization bill (H.R. 5136), stated the following in its discussion of the Navy's request for FY2011 funding for its research and development account:

> Future integrated nuclear power systems
>
> The budget request contained $366.5 million in PE 63570N[39] for advanced nuclear power systems, but contained no funds for development of small scale pressurized water reactors suitable for destroyer-sized vessels or for alternative nuclear power systems using thorium liquid salt technology.
> The committee remains committed to an all nuclear powered naval battle force. The committee notes that significant challenges in size and weight of nuclear technology make inclusion of integrated nuclear power systems on destroyer sized vessels currently impossible. Therefore, the committee believes that additional funding in engineering research and development is needed to design a smaller scale version of a naval pressurized water reactor, or to design a new reactor type potentially using a thorium liquid salt reactor developed for maritime use.
> The committee recommends an increase of $2.5 million in PE 63570N for research and design efforts to develop an integrated nuclear power system capable of use on destroyer-sized vessels either using a pressurized water reactor or a thorium liquid salt reactor. (Page 158)

Senate (S. 3454)

The Senate Armed Services Committee, in its report (S.Rept. 111-201 of June 4, 2010) on the FY2011 defense authorization bill (S. 3454), did not discuss the issue of nuclear power for surface ships other than aircraft carriers.

Final Version (H.R. 6523/P.L. 111-383)

The joint explanatory statement for the FY2011 defense authorization act (H.R. 6523/P.L. 111- 383 of January 7, 2011) did not discuss the issue of nuclear power for surface ships other than aircraft carriers.

FY2011 DOD Appropriations Bill (S. 3800)

Senate

The Senate Appropriations Committee, in its report (S.Rept. 111-295 of September 16, 2010) on S. 3800, did not discuss the issue of nuclear power for surface ships other than aircraft carriers.

PRIOR-YEAR LEGISLATIVE ACTIVITY

FY2010 Defense Authorization Act (H.R. 2647/P.L. 111-84)

House

The House Armed Services Committee, in its report (H.Rept. 111-166 of June 18, 2009) on H.R. 2647, stated:

> The committee believes that the next generation [CG(X)] cruiser must meet the challenge of emerging ballistic missile technology and that an integrated nuclear power system is required to achieve maximum capability of the vessel. (Page 72)

The report also stated:

> The committee remains committed to the direction of section 1012 of the National Defense Authorization Act for Fiscal Year 2008 (Public Law 110–181), which requires the use of an integrated nuclear propulsion system for the CGN(X) [cruiser]. (Page 75)

Section 246 of H.R. 2647 would require the Department of Defense (DOD) to submit to the congressional defense committees a study on the use of thorium-liquid fueled nuclear reactors for Navy surface ships. The text of Section 246 is as follows:

SEC. 246. STUDY ON THORIUM-LIQUID FUELED REACTORS FOR NAVAL FORCES.

(a) Study Required- The Secretary of Defense and the Chairman of the Joint Chiefs of Staff shall jointly carry out a study on the use of thorium-liquid fueled nuclear reactors for naval power needs pursuant to section 1012, of the National Defense Authorization Act for Fiscal Year 2008 (P.L. 110-181; 122 Stat. 303).

(b) Contents of Study- In carrying out the study required under subsection (a), the Secretary of Defense and the Chairman of the Joint Chiefs of Staff shall, with respect to naval power requirements for the Navy strike and amphibious force—

(1) compare and contrast thorium-liquid fueled reactor concept to the 2005 Quick Look, 2006 Navy Alternative Propulsion Study, and the navy CG(X) Analysis of Alternatives study;

(2) identify the benefits to naval operations which thorium-liquid fueled nuclear reactors or uranium reactors would provide to major surface combatants compared to conventionally fueled ships, including such benefits with respect to—

(A) fuel cycle, from mining to waste disposal;

(B) security of fuel supply;

(C) power needs for advanced weapons and sensors;

(D) safety of operation, waste handling and disposal, and proliferation issues compared to uranium reactors;

(E) no requirement to refuel and reduced logistics;

(F) ship upgrades and retrofitting;

(G) reduced manning;

(H) global range at flank speed, greater forward presence, and extended combat operations;

(I) power for advanced sensors and weapons, including electromagnetic guns and lasers;

(J) survivability due to increased performance and reduced signatures;

(K) high power density propulsion;

(L) operational tempo;

(M) operational effectiveness; and

(N) estimated cost-effectiveness; and

(3) conduct a ROM cost-effectiveness comparison of nuclear reactors in use by the Navy as of the date of the enactment of this Act, thorium-

liquid fueled reactors, and conventional fueled major surface combatants, which shall include a comparison of—
    (A) security, safety, and infrastructure costs of fuel supplies;
    (B) nuclear proliferation issues;
    (C) reactor safety;
    (D) nuclear fuel safety, waste handling, and storage;
    (E) power requirements and distribution for sensors, weapons, and propulsion; and
    (F) capabilities to fully execute the Navy Maritime Strategic Concept.
    (c) Report- Not later than February 1, 2011, the Secretary of Defense and the Chairman of the Joint Chiefs of Staff shall jointly submit to the congressional defense committees a report on the results of the study required under subsection (a).

Senate

Section 1012 of the FY2010 defense authorization bill (S. 1390) as reported by the Senate Armed Services Committee (S.Rept. 111-35 of July 2, 2009) would repeal Section 1012 of the FY2008 defense authorization act (H.R. 4986/P.L. 110-181 of January 28, 2008). The committee's report stated:

> The committee recommends a provision [Section 1012] that would repeal section 1012 of the National Defense Authorization Act for Fiscal Year 2008 (P.L. 110-181).
> Section 1012 of the National Defense Authorization Act for Fiscal Year 2008 (P.L. 110- 181), as amended by section 1015 of the Duncan Hunter National Defense Authorization Act for Fiscal Year 2009 (P.L. 110-417), would require that all new classes of surface combatants and all new amphibious assault ships larger than 15,000 deadweight ton light ship displacement have integrated nuclear power systems, unless the Secretary of Defense determines that the inclusion of an integrated nuclear power system in such vessel is not in the national interest.
> The committee believes that the Navy is already having too much difficulty in achieving the goal of a 313-ship fleet without adding a substantial increment to the acquisition price of a significant portion of the fleet. Moreover, current acquisition law and the Weapon System Acquisition Reform Act of 2009 (P.L. 111-23) emphasize the need to start acquisition programs on a sure footing as a central mechanism by which the Department of Defense (DOD) can get control of cost growth and schedule slippage on major defense acquisition programs. Therefore, Congress should be loathe to dictate a particular outcome of a requirements process before the Department has conducted the normal requirements review.

The committee expects that the Navy will continue to evaluate the integrated nuclear power alternative for any new class of major surface combatants, but would prefer that any Navy requirements analysis not be skewed toward a particular outcome. (Page 170)

Conference

The conference report (H.Rept. 111-288 of October 7, 2009) on H.R. 2647/P.L. 111-84 of October 28, 2009, stated:

> Repeal of policy relating to the major combatant vessels of the Unites States Navy
>
> The Senate amendment contained a provision (sec. 1012) that would repeal section 1012 of the National Defense Authorization Act for Fiscal Year 2008 (Public Law 110–181). Section 1012, as amended, would require that all new classes of surface combatants and all new amphibious assault ships larger than 15,000 deadweight ton light ship displacement have integrated nuclear power systems, unless the Secretary of Defense determines that the inclusion of an integrated nuclear power system in such vessel is not in the national interest.
>
> The House bill contained no similar provision.
>
> The Senate recedes. (Page 822)

The report also stated:

> Study on thorium-liquid fueled reactors for Naval forces
>
> The House bill contained a provision (sec. 246) that would have directed the Secretary of Defense and the Chairman of the Joint Chiefs of Staff to carry out jointly a study on the use of thorium-liquid fueled nuclear reactors for naval propulsion.
>
> The Senate amendment contained no similar provision.
>
> The House recedes.
>
> The conferees note that while there may be credible research initiatives to explore the use of molten salt reactors for commercial power generation, the use of molten salt reactors on naval vessels is not currently technically feasible and a requirement to perform a study on the use of molten salt reactors is premature. This is due to technology challenges with material construction (molten salt reactors are inherently corrosive to metals), storage of the liquid fuel, and radiation shielding for the crew from a non-solid fuel reactor. The conferees recommend that the Navy continue to monitor the progress of technology development in

commercial application of molten salt reactors, including licensing, for potential future application. (Page 708)

FY2009 Defense Authorization Act (H.R. 5658/P.L. 110-417)

House

The House-reported version of H.R. 5658 contained a provision (Section 1013) that would amend Section 1012 of the FY2008 defense authorization act (see discussion below) to include amphibious ships and amphibious command ships of a certain minimum size as among the types of ships to be built in the future with nuclear power unless the Secretary of Defense notifies Congress that nuclear power for a given class of ship would not be in the national interest. Section 1013 stated:

> SEC. 1013. POLICY RELATING TO MAJOR COMBATANT VESSELS OF THE STRIKE FORCES OF THE UNITED STATES NAVY.
> Section 1012(c)(1) of the National Defense Authorization Act for Fiscal Year 2008 (P.L. 110-181) is amended by adding at the end the following:
> '(D) Amphibious assault ships, including dock landing ships (LSD), amphibious transport-dock ships (LPD), helicopter assault ships (LHA/LHD), and amphibious command ships (LCC), if such vessels exceed 15,000 dead weight ton light ship displacement.'[40]

In its report (H.Rept. 110-652 of May 16, 2008) on H.R. 5658, the House Armed Services Committee stated:

> This section would amend section 1012 of the National Defense Authorization Act for Fiscal Year 2008 (P.L. 110-181) by requiring that in addition to future ship classes of aircraft carriers, major surface combatants, and submarines, that assault echelon amphibious ships also must be constructed with integrated nuclear power systems if the ship's light weight displacement is greater than 15 thousand tons.[41]
> The committee believes the future naval force should not be reliant on the availability of fossil fuel for fleet operations. Removing the need for access to fossil fuel sources significantly multiplies the effectiveness of the entire battle force and eliminates the dependence on foreign nation support of deployed naval forces. (Pages 428-429)

Senate

The report of the Senate Armed Services Committee (S.Rept. 110-335 of May 12, 2008) on the FY2009 defense authorization bill (S. 3001) stated, with regard to the CG(X) cruiser, that:

> The John Warner National Defense Authorization Act for Fiscal Year 2007 (P.L. 109-364) required that the Navy include nuclear power in its Analysis of Alternatives (AoA) for the CG(X) propulsion system.
> Section 1012 of the National Defense Authorization Act for Fiscal Year 2008 (P.L. 110-181) further requires that CG(X) be nuclear powered, unless the Secretary of Defense submits a notification that inclusion of an integrated nuclear power system is not in the national interest. The statement of managers accompanying that act directed the Secretary of the Navy to submit a report with the budget request for fiscal year 2009 providing information regarding CG(X) design, cost, schedule, industrial base considerations, and risk assessment; that would reflect the results of the CG(X) AoA and provide evidence that the Navy is on schedule for procuring the first ship of the class in 2011.
> The Secretary of the Navy has delayed submission of the CG(X) report because the CG(X) AoA, which was scheduled to be complete by third quarter fiscal year 2007, remains under review by the Navy. Fundamental considerations regarding the cruiser's requirements, characteristics, technology readiness levels, and affordability continue to be studied, making it likely that milestone A, which was targeted for September 2007, will slip into 2009. By all measures, there is no reasonable path for the next-generation cruiser to meet the current schedule for milestone B and award of a ship construction contract in 2011.
> Pending completion of the AoA, determination of radar requirements, ship characteristics, propulsion system, and an executable program schedule, and in view of the delay to program major milestones, the activities planned for fiscal years 2008 and 2009 cannot be executed per the schedule reflected in the fiscal year 2009 budget request. Therefore, the committee recommends a decrease [in the Navy's request for FY2009 research and development funding] of $87.2 million in PE 64300N and a decrease of $33.6 million in PE 64501N. These recommended decreases would maintain the cruiser development activities at the same level as was funded in fiscal year 2008. (Page 195)

Compromise

In lieu of a conference report, there was a compromise version of S. 3001 that was accompanied by a joint explanatory statement. Section 4 of S. 3001 states that the joint explanatory statement "shall have the same effect with respect to the implementation of this Act as if it were a joint explanatory statement of a committee of conference." S. 3001 was signed into law as P.L. 110- 417 on October 14, 2008.

Section 1015 of S. 3001/P.L. 110-417 amended Section 1012 of the FY2008 defense authorization act (see discussion below) to include amphibious ships and amphibious command ships of a certain minimum size as among the types of ships to be built in the future with nuclear power unless the Secretary of Defense notifies Congress that nuclear power for a given class of ship would not be in the national interest. Section 1015 states:

> SEC. 1015. POLICY RELATING TO MAJOR COMBATANT VESSELS OF THE STRIKE FORCES OF THE UNITED STATES NAVY.
> Section 1012(c)(1) of the National Defense Authorization Act for Fiscal Year 2008 (P.L. 110-181) is amended by adding at the end the following:
> "(D) Amphibious assault ships, including dock landing ships (LSD), amphibious trans port— dock ships (LPD), helicopter assault ships (LHA/LHD), and amphibious command ships (LCC), if such vessels exceed 15,000 dead weight ton light ship displacement."[42]

FY2008 Defense Authorization Act (H.R. 4986/P.L. 110-181)

House

The House-reported version of the FY2008 defense authorization bill (originally H.R. 1585, a bill that was succeeded by H.R. 4986 following a presidential veto of H.R. 1585) contained a provision (Section 1012) that would make it U.S. policy to build submarines, aircraft carriers, cruisers, and other large surface combatants with nuclear power unless the Secretary of Defense notifies Congress that nuclear power for a given class of ship would not be in the national interest. The provision stated:

> SEC. 1012. POLICY RELATING TO MAJOR COMBATANT VESSELS OF THE STRIKE FORCES OF THE UNITED STATES NAVY.
> (a) Integrated Nuclear Power Systems- It is the policy of the United States to construct the major combatant vessels of the strike forces of the United States Navy, including all new classes of such vessels, with integrated nuclear power systems.

(b) Requirement to Request Nuclear Vessels- If a request is submitted to Congress in the budget for a fiscal year for construction of a new class of major combatant vessel for the strike forces of the United States, the request shall be for such a vessel with an integrated nuclear power system, unless the Secretary of Defense submits with the request a notification to Congress that the inclusion of an integrated nuclear power system in such vessel is not in the national interest.

(c) Definitions- In this section:

(1) MAJOR COMBATANT VESSELS OF THE STRIKE FORCES OF THE UNITED STATES NAVY- The term 'major combatant vessels of the strike forces of the United States Navy' means the following:

(A) Submarines.

(B) Aircraft carriers.

(C) Cruisers, battleships, or other large surface combatants whose primary mission includes protection of carrier strike groups, expeditionary strike groups, and vessels comprising a sea base.

(2) INTEGRATED NUCLEAR POWER SYSTEM- The term 'integrated nuclear power system' means a ship engineering system that uses a naval nuclear reactor as its energy source and generates sufficient electric energy to provide power to the ship's electrical loads, including its combat systems and propulsion motors.

(3) BUDGET- The term 'budget' means the budget that is submitted to Congress by the President under section 1105(a) of title 31, United States Code.

The House Armed Services Committee, in its report (H.Rept. 110-146 of May 11, 2007) on H.R. 1585, stated the following in regard to Section 1012:

> This section would require that all new ship classes of submarines, cruisers, and aircraft carriers be built with nuclear power systems unless the Secretary of Defense notifies the committee that it is not in the national interest to do so.
>
> The committee believes that the mobility, endurance, and electric power generation capability of nuclear powered warships is essential to the next generation of Navy cruisers. The Navy's report to Congress on alternative propulsion methods for surface combatants and amphibious warfare ships, required by section 130 of the National Defense Authorization Act for Fiscal Year 2006 (P.L. 109-163), indicated that the total lifecycle cost for medium-sized nuclear surface combatants is equivalent to conventionally powered ships. The committee notes that this study only compared acquisition and maintenance costs and did not analyze the increased speed and endurance capability of nuclear powered vessels.

The committee believes that the primary escort vessels for the Navy's fleet of aircraft carriers should have the same speed and endurance capability as the aircraft carrier. The committee also notes that surface combatants with nuclear propulsion systems would be more capable during independent operations because there would be no need for underway fuel replenishment. (Page 387)

Senate

The Senate-reported version of the FY2008 defense authorization bill (S. 1547) did not contain a provision analogous to Section 1012 of the House-reported version of H.R. 1585. The report of the Senate Armed Services Committee on S. 1547 (S.Rept. 110-77 of June 5, 2007) did not comment directly on the issue of nuclear power for Navy ships other than submarines and aircraft carriers.

Conference

Section 1012 of the conference report (H.Rept. 110-477 of December 6, 2007) on H.R. 1585 is the same as Section 1012 of the House-reported version of H.R. 1585 (see discussion above). In discussing Section 1012, the conference report stated:

> The Navy's next opportunity to apply this guidance will be the next generation cruiser, or "CG(X)". Under the current future-years defense program (FYDP), the Navy plans to award the construction contract for CG(X) in fiscal year 2011. Under this provision, the next cruiser would be identified as "CGN(X)" to designate the ship as nuclear powered. Under the Navy's normal shipbuilding schedule for the two programs that already have nuclear power systems (aircraft carriers and submarines), the Navy seeks authorization and appropriations for long lead time nuclear components for ships 2 years prior to full authorization and appropriation for construction.
>
> The conferees recognize that the milestone decision for the Navy's CG(X) is only months away. After that milestone decision, the Navy and its contractors will begin a significant design effort, and, in that process, will be making significant tradeoff decisions and discarding major options (such as propulsion alternatives). This is the normal process for the Navy and the Department of Defense (DOD) to make choices that will lead to producing a contract design that will be the basis for awarding the construction contract for the lead ship in 2011.
>
> In order for the Navy to live by the spirit of this guidance, the conferees agree that:
>
> (1) the Navy would be required to proceed through the contract design phase of the program with a comprehensive effort to design a

CGN(X) independent of the outcome of decisions that the Navy or the DOD will make at the next milestone decision point regarding any preferred propulsion system for the next generation cruiser;

(2) if the Navy intends to maintain the schedule in the current FYDP and award a vessel in fiscal year 2011, the Navy would need to request advance procurement for nuclear components in the fiscal year 2009 budget request; and

(3) the Navy must consider options for:

(a) maintaining the segment of the industrial base that currently produces the conventionally powered destroyer and amphibious forces of the Navy;

(b) certifying yards which comprise that segment of the industrial base to build nuclear-powered vessels; or

(c) seeking other alternatives for building non-nuclear ships in the future if the Navy is only building nuclear-powered surface combatant ships for some period of time as it builds CGN(X) vessels; and

(d) identifying sources of funds to pay for the additional near-term costs of the integrated nuclear power system, either from offsets within the Navy's budget, from elsewhere within the Department's resources, or from gaining additional funds for DOD overall.

The conferees recognize that these considerations will require significant additional near-term investment by the Navy. Some in the Navy have asserted that, despite such added investment, the Navy would not be ready to award a shipbuilding contract for a CGN(X) in fiscal year 2011 as in the current FYDP.

Section 128 of the John Warner National Defense Authorization Act for Fiscal Year 2007 (Public Law 109-364) required that the Navy include nuclear power in its Analysis of Alternatives (AOA) for the CG(X) propulsion system. The conferees are aware that the CG(X) AOA is nearing completion, in which case the Navy should have some indications of what it will require to design and construct a CGN(X) class.

Accordingly, the conferees direct the Secretary of the Navy to submit a report to the congressional defense committees with the budget request for fiscal year 2009 providing the following information:

(1) the set of next generation cruiser characteristics, such as displacement and manning, which would be affected by the requirement for including an integrated nuclear power system;

(2) the Navy's estimate for additional costs to develop, design, and construct a CGN(X) to fill the requirement for the next generation cruiser, and the optimal phasing of those costs in order to deliver CGN(X) most affordably;

(3) the Navy's assessment of any effects on the delivery schedule for the first ship of the next generation cruiser class that would be associated with shifting the design to incorporate an integrated nuclear propulsion

system, options for reducing or eliminating those schedule effects, and alternatives for meeting next generation cruiser requirements during any intervening period if the cruiser's full operational capability were delayed;

(4) the Navy's estimate for the cost associated with certifying those shipyards that currently produce conventionally powered surface combatants, to be capable of constructing and integrating a nuclear-powered combatant;

(5) any other potential effects on the Navy's 30-year shipbuilding plan as a result of implementing these factors;

(6) such other considerations that would need to be addressed in parallel with design and construction of a CGN(X) class, including any unique test and training facilities, facilities and infrastructure requirements for potential CGN(X) homeports, and environmental assessments that may require long-term coordination and planning; and

(7) an assessment of the highest risk areas associated with meeting this requirement, and the Navy's alternatives for mitigating such risk. (Pages 984-986)

H.R. 1585 was vetoed by the President on December 28, 2007. In response, Congress passed a modified bill, H.R. 4986, that took into account the President's objections to H.R. 1585. The modifications incorporated into H.R. 4986 did not affect the provisions discussed here, and for these and other unmodified parts of the bill, H.Rept. 110-477 in effect serves as the conference report for H.R. 4986. H.R. 4986 was signed into law as P.L. 110-181 on January 28, 2008.

Section 1012 of the conference report is similar in some respects to the so-called Title VIII legislation of the 1970s that required future Navy ships of certain kinds to be nuclear-powered.[43]

FY2006 Defense Authorization Act (H.R. 1815/P.L. 109-163)

Section 130 of the conference report (H.Rept. 109-360 of December 18, 2005) on the FY2006 defense authorization act (H.R. 1815/P.L. 109-163 of January 6, 2006) required the Navy to submit a report by November 1, 2006, on alternative propulsion methods for surface combatants and amphibious warfare ships. The Navy submitted the report to Congress in January 2007. Section 130 states:

SEC. 130. REPORT ON ALTERNATIVE PROPULSION METHODS FOR SURFACE COMBATANTS AND AMPHIBIOUS WARFARE SHIPS.

(a) ANALYSIS OF ALTERNATIVES.—The Secretary of the Navy shall conduct an analysis of alternative propulsion methods for surface combatant vessels and amphibious warfare ships of the Navy.

(b) REPORT.—The Secretary shall submit to the congressional defense committees a report on the analysis of alternative propulsion systems carried out under subsection (a). The report shall be submitted not later than November 1, 2006.

(c) MATTERS TO BE INCLUDED.—The report under subsection (b) shall include the following:

(1) The key assumptions used in carrying out the analysis under subsection (a).

(2) The methodology and techniques used in conducting the analysis.

(3) A description of current and future technology relating to propulsion that has been incorporated in recently-designed surface combatant vessels and amphibious warfare ships or that is expected to be available for those types of vessels within the next 10-to-20 years.

(4) A description of each propulsion alternative for surface combatant vessels and amphibious warfare ships that was considered under the study and an analysis and evaluation of each such alternative from an operational and cost-effectiveness standpoint.

(5) A comparison of the life-cycle costs of each propulsion alternative.

(6) For each nuclear propulsion alternative, an analysis of when that nuclear propulsion alternative becomes cost effective as the price of a barrel of crude oil increases for each type of ship.

(7) The conclusions and recommendations of the study, including those conclusions and recommendations that could impact the design of future ships or lead to modifications of existing ships.

(8) The Secretary's intended actions, if any, for implementation of the conclusions and recommendations of the study.

(d) LIFE-CYCLE COSTS.—For purposes of this section, the term "life-cycle costs" includes those elements of cost that would be considered for a life-cycle cost analysis for a major defense acquisition program.

End Notes

[1] For more on the CG(X) program and its proposed cancellation, see CRS Report RL34179, *Navy CG(X) Cruiser Program: Background for Congress*, by Ronald O'Rourke; and CRS Report RL32109, *Navy DDG-51 and DDG-1000 Destroyer Programs: Background and Issues for Congress*, by Ronald O'Rourke.

[2] U.S. Navy nuclear-powered ships use pressurized water reactors (PWRs) that are fueled with highly enriched uranium. In a PWR, water flowing through the reactor is heated by the nuclear fuel to a high temperature. The water is pressurized (maintained at a high pressure) so that it does not boil as it heats up. A heat exchanger is then used to transfer heat from the radioactive pressurized water to a separate circuit of non-radioactive water. As the non-radioactive water heats up, it turns into steam that is used to power turbines that drive the ship's propellers and generate power for shipboard equipment. A small number of non-military ships have been built with nuclear power in recent decades, including the U.S.-built commercial cargo ship NS Savannah, three other commercial cargo ships built in Germany, Japan, and the Soviet Union, and several Soviet/Russian-built nuclear-powered icebreakers. The four cargo ships are no longer in service. More recently, the Center for the Commercial Deployment of Transportation Technologies (CCDoTT) of California State University, Long Beach, has examined the potential cost-effectiveness of building a new generation of nuclear-powered commercial cargo ships.

[3] For an aircraft carrier, the use of nuclear power permits space inside the ship that would have been used for storing ship fuel to be used instead for storing aircraft fuel or other supplies. This lengthens the period of time that a carrier can sustain aircraft operations before needing to take on fuel or other supplies.

[4] See also 42 USC 7158. [5] The Navy's final three non-nuclear-powered combat submarines were procured in FY1956, entered service in 1959, retired in 1988-1990. A non-nuclear-powered, non-combat auxiliary research submarine, the Dolphin (AGSS-555), was procured in FY1961, entered service in 1968, and retired in January 2007.

[5] The Navy's final three non-nuclear-powered combat submarines were procured in FY1956, entered service in 1959, retired in 1988-1990. A non-nuclear-powered, non-combat auxiliary research submarine, the Dolphin (AGSS-555), was procured in FY1961, entered service in 1968, and retired in January 2007.

[6] Source: Telephone conversation with Naval Reactors, March 8, 2007. Naval Reactor states that the cost figure of about $660 million for an aircraft carrier ($330 million for each of two fuel cores) applies to both existing Nimitz (CVN-68) class carriers and the new Gerald R. Ford (CVN-78) class carrier (also known as the CVN-21 class).

[7] For more on the CG(X) program, see CRS Report RL34179, *Navy CG(X) Cruiser Program: Background for Congress*, by Ronald O'Rourke.

[8] The FY2009 budget called for procuring the first CG(X) in FY2011, but the Navy's proposed FY2010 budget deferred the planned procurement of the first CG(X) beyond FY2015.

[9] For more on Navy BMD programs, see CRS Report RL33745, *Navy Aegis Ballistic Missile Defense (BMD) Program: Background and Issues for Congress*, by Ronald O'Rourke.

[10] Source: Testimony of Navy officials to the Seapower and Expeditionary Forces Subcommittee of the House Armed Services Committee, March 1, 2007.

[11] Source: Testimony of Navy officials to the Seapower and Expeditionary Forces Subcommittee of the House Armed Services Committee, March 1, 2007.

[12] For more on the CVN-21 program, see CRS Report RS20643, *Navy Ford (CVN-78) Class Aircraft Carrier Program: Background and Issues for Congress*, by Ronald O'Rourke.

[13] For more on the CG(X) program and its proposed cancellation, see CRS Report RL34179, *Navy CG(X) Cruiser Program: Background for Congress*, by Ronald O'Rourke; and CRS Report RL32109, *Navy DDG-51 and DDG-1000 Destroyer Programs: Background and Issues for Congress*, by Ronald O'Rourke.

[14] The five yards are the Portsmouth Naval Shipyard of Kittery, ME; the Mare Island Naval Shipyard of Mare Island, CA; the Ingalls shipyard of Pascagoula, MS, that now forms part

of Northrop Grumman Ship Systems; Bethlehem Steel of Quincy, MA (which became a part of General Dynamics); and New York Shipbuilding of Camden, NJ.

[15] Ingalls built its nuclear-powered submarines at its older East Bank facility. Ingalls' newer West Bank facility has been used for building conventionally powered surface ships, principally surface combatants and large-deck amphibious ships.

[16] In addition to building 12 nuclear-powered submarines, Northrop Grumman states that Ingalls' facilities "allowed Ingalls to participate in submarine overhaul and refueling. By the time the shipyard's nuclear facility was decommissioned in 1980, 11 U.S. Navy attack submarines had been overhauled and/or refueled at Ingalls." Source: Northrop Grumman chronological perspective on Northrop Grumman Ship Systems, at http://www.ss.northropgrumman.com/company/chronological.html.

[17] U.S. Naval Nuclear Propulsion Program, briefing entitled "Nuclear and Fossil Fuel Powered Surface Ships, Quick Look Analysis," presented to CRS on March 22, 2006. The analysis concluded that total life-cycle costs for nuclear-powered versions of large-deck aircraft carriers, LHA-type amphibious assault ships and surface combatants would equal those of conventionally powered versions when the price of diesel fuel marine (DFM) delivered to the Navy reached $55, $80, and $205 per barrel, respectively. Since the cost of DFM delivered to the Navy was calculated to be roughly 15% greater than that of crude oil, these figures corresponded to break-even crude-oil costs of about $48, $70, and $178 per barrel, respectively.

[18] In each case, the cost increase is for the fifth ship in a class being built at two shipyards.

[19] Source: Statement of The Honorable Dr. Delores M. Etter, Assistant Secretary of the Navy (Research, Development and Acquisition), et al., Before the Seapower and Expeditionary Forces Subcommittee of the House Armed Services Committee on Integrated Nuclear Power Systems for Future Naval Surface Combatants, March 1, 2007, pp. 4-5.

[20] The Navy in 2007 estimated that follow-on DDG-1000 destroyers would cost an average of about $1.9 billion each to procure in constant FY2007 dollars. (This figure was based on the then-year costs for the third through seventh ships in the DDG-1000 class, which the Navy wants to procure in FY2009-FY2013. These costs were converted into constant FY2007 dollars using a January 2007 Navy shipbuilding deflator. The deflator was provided by the Navy to the Congressional Budget Office, which forwarded it to CRS.) Increasing a ship's procurement cost from about $1.9 billion to $2.5 billion or $2.6 billion (i.e., increasing it by $600 million to $700 million) equates to an increase of 32% to 37%.

[21] Statement of Admiral Kirkland H. Donald, U.S. Navy, Director, Naval Nuclear Propulsion Program, Before the House Armed Services Committee Seapower and Expeditionary Forces Subcommittee on Nuclear Propulsion For Surface Ships, March 1, 2007, p. 13.

[22] Spoken testimony of Admiral Kirkland Donald before the Seapower and Expeditionary Forces Subcommittee of the House Armed Services Committee, March 1, 2007.

[23] Testimony of Winfred Nash, President, BWXT, Nuclear Operations Division, Before the Subcommittee on Seapower and Expeditionary Forces of the House Armed Service Committee [on Submarine Force Structure and Acquisition Policy], March 8, 2007, pp. 2 and 4.

[24] For a standard U.S. government projection of future oil prices, assuming current policy remains in place, see the Energy Information Administration's Annual Energy Outlook, at http://www.eia.doe.gov/oiaf/aeo/index.html.

[25] See, for example, the remarks of Representative Taylor at the hearing of the Seapower and Expeditionary Forces Subcommittee of the House Armed Services Committee, March 1, 2007.

[26] Source: Testimony of Navy officials to the Seapower and Expeditionary Forces Subcommittee of the House Armed Services Committee, March 1, 2007.

[27] Spoken testimony of Vice Admiral Jonathan Greenert before the Seapower and Expeditionary Forces Subcommittee of the House Armed Services Committee, March 1, 2007.

[28] See, for example, the discussion of the issue at http://www.utilipoint.com/issuealert/print.asp?id=1728.

[29] For examples of articles discussing the idea of using nuclear-powered ships to generate electrical power for use ashore, see Jose Femenia, "Nuclear Ships Can Help Meet U.S. Electrical Needs," *U.S. Naval Institute Proceedings*, August 2004: 78-80; and Linda de France, "Using Navy Nuclear Reactors To Help Power California Not Worth Effort," *Aerospace Daily*, May 4, 2001.

[30] Spoken testimony of Admiral Kirkland Donald before the Seapower and Expeditionary Forces Subcommittee of the House Armed Services Committee, March 1, 2007.

[31] Statement of Admiral Kirkland H. Donald, U.S. Navy, Director, Naval Nuclear Propulsion Program, Before the House Armed Services Committee Seapower and Expeditionary Forces Subcommittee on Nuclear Propulsion For Surface Ships, March 1, 2007, p. 13.

[32] Source: Statement of The Honorable Dr. Delores M. Etter, Assistant Secretary of the Navy (Research, Development and Acquisition), et al., Before the Seapower and Expeditionary Forces Subcommittee of the House Armed Services Committee on Integrated Nuclear Power Systems for Future Naval Surface Combatants, March 1, 2007, p. 7.

[33] Spoken testimony of Admiral Kirkland Donald before the Seapower and Expeditionary Forces Subcommittee of the House Armed Services Committee, March 1, 2007.

[34] Spoken testimony of Vice Admiral Paul E. Sullivan, Commander, Naval Sea Systems Command, to the Seapower and Expeditionary Forces Subcommittee of the House Armed Services Committee, March 1, 2007.

[35] Spoken testimony of Admiral Kirkland Donald before the Seapower and Expeditionary Forces Subcommittee of the House Armed Services Committee, March 1, 2007.

[36] The Enterprise has a one-of-a-kind, eight-reactor nuclear power plant that creates training demands unique to that ship.

[37] Spoken testimony of Admiral Kirkland Donald before the Seapower and Expeditionary Forces Subcommittee of the House Armed Services Committee, March 1, 2007.

[38] Spoken testimony of Admiral Kirkland Donald before the Seapower and Expeditionary Forces Subcommittee of the House Armed Services Committee, March 1, 2007.

[39] Line items in Department of Defense (DOD) research and development accounts are called program elements, or PEs.

[40] The sizes of commercial ships are often expressed in deadweight tons, while the sizes of Navy combatant ships are usually expressed in terms of full load or light ship displacement. The terms deadweight tons and light ship displacement are not normally joined together to form a single expression of a ship's size. When joined together, the two terms can be viewed as being in tension with one another, since the first refers to the weight of a ship's cargo, fuel, water, stores, and other loads, while the second refers to the weight of a ship without these loads.

[41] This report language, which refers to light weight displacement but not to deadweight tons, suggests that the inclusion of the words "dead weight ton" in the Section 1013 might be a printing error.

[42] The inclusion of the words "dead weight ton" in this section might be a printing error; see the previous two footnotes for a discussion.

[43] The Title VIII legislation comprised Sections 801-804 of the FY1975 defense authorization act (H.R. 14592/P.L. 93- 365, August 5, 1974, 88 Stat. 408-409). The legislation was codified at 10 USC 7291. Section 801 made it U.S. policy "to modernize the strike forces of the United States Navy by the construction of nuclear-powered major combatant vessels and to provide for an adequate industrial base for the research, development, design, construction, operation, and maintenance for such vessels." Section 801 also stated: "New construction major combatant vessels for the strike forces of the United States Navy authorized subsequent to the date of enactment of this Act becomes law [sic] shall be nuclear powered, except as provided in this title." Section 802 defined the term "major combatant vessels for the strike forces of the United States Navy." Section 803 required the Secretary of Defense to submit a report to Congress each year, along with the annual budget request, on the application of nuclear power to such ships. Section 804 stated that "All requests for authorizations or appropriations from Congress" for such ships shall be for construction of nuclear-powered versions of such ships "unless and until the President has fully advised the Congress that construction of nuclear powered vessels for such purpose is not in the national interest," in which case the President is to provide, for Congress' consideration, an alternate program of nuclear-powered ships, with appropriate design, cost, and schedule information. Title VIII was repealed by Section 810 of the FY1979 defense authorization act (S. 3486/P.L. 95-485, October 20, 1978, 92 Stat. 1623). Section 810 of that act replaced the Title VIII legislation with a policy statement on Navy shipbuilding policy that did not mandate the use of nuclear power for any Navy ships. Section 810, like the Title VIII legislation, was codified at 10 USC 7291. It was subsequently recodified at 10 USC 7310, pursuant to a law (H.R. 4623/P.L. 97-295 of October 12, 1982) that amended titles 10, 14, 37, and 38 to codify recent law. 10 USC 7310 was then repealed by Section 824(a)(8) of the FY1994 defense authorization act (H.R. 2401/P.L. 103-160 of November 30, 1993).

In: Navy Nuclear-Powered Surface Ships
Editors: R. Cabitta, M. Rocello

ISBN: 978-1-61470-790-5
© 2011 Nova Science Publishers, Inc.

Chapter 2

THE COST-EFFECTIVENESS OF NUCLEAR POWER FOR NAVY SURFACE SHIPS[*]

Congress of the United States,
Congressional Budget Office

PREFACE

In recent years, the Congress has shown interest in powering some of the Navy's future destroyers and amphibious warfare ships with nuclear rather than conventional (petroleum-based) fuel. At the request of the former Chairman of the Subcommittee on Seapower and Projection Forces of the House Committee on Armed Services, the Congressional Budget Office (CBO) has estimated the difference in life-cycle costs (the total costs incurred for a ship, from acquisition through operations to disposal) between powering those new surface ships with nuclear reactors and equipping them with conventional engines.

R. Derek Trunkey and Matthew Goldberg of CBO's National Security Division wrote the study under the general supervision of J. Michael Gilmore (formerly of CBO) and David Mosher. Eric J. Labs, also of the National Security Division, provided projections of the Navy's future fleets. Raymond Hall of CBO's Budget Analysis Division prepared the estimates of acquisition costs under the general supervision of Sarah Jennings. Ron Gecan, Heidi Golding, Deborah Lucas, Damien Moore,

---

[*] This is an edited, reformatted and augmented version of a Congress of the United States, Congressional Budget Office publication, dated May 2011.

Dawn Sauter Regan, and Jason Wheelock, all of CBO, contributed to the analysis, and Ron Gecan and Steven Weinberg developed CBO's forecasts of oil prices. Donald Birchler of the CNA Corporation reviewed the study. (The assistance of an external reviewer implies no responsibility for the final product, which rests solely with CBO.)

Leah Mazade edited the study, Christine Bogusz proofread it, and Jeanine Rees prepared it for publication. Maureen Costantino designed the cover. Monte Ruffin produced the initial print copies, Linda Schimmel coordinated the print distribution, and Simone Thomas prepared the electronic version for CBO's Web site (www.cbo.gov).

Douglas W. Elmendorf
Director

SUMMARY AND INTRODUCTION

The U.S. Navy plans to build a number of new surface ships in the coming decades, according to its most recent 30-year shipbuilding plan.[1] All of the Navy's aircraft carriers (and submarines) are powered by nuclear reactors; its other surface combatants are powered by engines that use conventional petroleum-based fuels. The Navy could save money on fuel in the future by purchasing additional nuclear-powered ships rather than conventionally powered ships. Those savings in fuel costs, however, would be offset by the additional up-front costs required for the procurement of nuclear-powered ships.

To assess the relative costs of using nuclear versus conventional propulsion for ships other than carriers and submarines, the Congressional Budget Office (CBO) developed a hypothetical future fleet, based on the Navy's shipbuilding plan, of new destroyers and amphibious warfare ships that are candidates for nuclear propulsion systems. Specifically, CBO chose for its analysis the Navy's planned new version of the DDG-51 destroyer and its replacement, the DDG(X); the LH(X) amphibious assault ship; and the LSD(X) amphibious dock landing ship. CBO then estimated the life-cycle costs for each ship in that fleet—that is, the costs over the ship's entire 40-year service life, beginning with its acquisition and progressing through the annual expenditures over 40 years for its fuel, personnel, and other operations and support and, finally, its disposal. CBO compared life-cycle costs under two alternative versions of the fleet: Each version comprised the same number of

The Cost-Effectiveness of Nuclear Power for Navy Surface Ships 41

ships of each class but differed in whether the ships were powered by conventional systems that used petroleum-based fuels or by nuclear reactors.

Estimates of the relative costs of using nuclear power versus conventional fuels for ships depend in large part on the projected path of oil prices, which determine how much the Navy must pay for fuel in the future. The initial costs for building and fueling a nuclear-powered ship are greater than those for building a conventionally powered ship. However, once the Navy has acquired a nuclear ship, it incurs no further costs for fuel. If oil prices rose substantially in the future, the estimated savings in fuel costs from using nuclear power over a ship's lifetime could offset the higher initial costs to procure the ship. In recent years, oil prices have shown considerable volatility; for example, the average price of all crude oil delivered to U.S. refiners peaked at about $130 per barrel in June and July 2008, then declined substantially, and has risen significantly again, to more than $100 per barrel in March of this year.

CBO regularly projects oil prices for 10-year periods as part of the macroeconomic forecast that underlies the baseline budget projections that the agency publishes each year.[2] In its January 2011 macroeconomic projections, CBO estimated that oil prices would average $86 per barrel in 2011 and over the next decade would grow at an average rate of about 1 percentage point per year above the rate of general inflation, reaching $95 per barrel (in 2011 dollars) by 2021.[3] After 2021, CBO assumes, the price will continue to grow at a rate of 1 percentage point above inflation, reaching $114 per barrel (in 2011 dollars) by 2040.[4]

If oil prices followed that trajectory, total life-cycle costs for a nuclear fleet would be 19 percent higher than those for a conventional fleet, in CBO's estimation. Specifically, total life-cycle costs would be 19 percent higher for a fleet of nuclear destroyers, 4 percent higher for a fleet of nuclear LH(X) amphibious assault ships, and 33 percent higher for a fleet of nuclear LSD(X) amphibious dock landing ships.

To determine how sensitive those findings are to the trajectory of oil prices, CBO also examined a case in which oil prices start from a value of $86 per barrel in 2011 and then rise at a rate higher than the real (inflation-adjusted) growth of 1 percent in CBO's baseline trajectory. That analysis suggested that a fleet of nuclear-powered destroyers would become cost-effective if the real annual rate of growth of oil prices exceeded 3.4 percent—which implies oil prices of $223 or more per barrel (in 2011 dollars) in 2040. Similarly, a fleet of nuclear LH(X) amphibious assault ships would become cost-effective if oil prices grew at a real annual rate of 1.7 percent, implying a price of $140 per barrel of oil in 2040—about the same price that was reached in 2008 but not sustained for any length of time. A fleet of nuclear LSD(X) amphibious dock landing ships would become cost-effective at real annual growth rate of 4.7 percent, or a price in 2040 of $323 per barrel.

In addition to the uncertain future path of oil prices, questions remain about the amount of energy that the new surface ships will use, which could be substantially higher or lower than projected. Energy usage is a particularly significant factor for ships such as destroyers that require large amounts of energy for purposes other than propulsion. Employing an approach similar to that used to assess sensitivity to oil prices, CBO estimated that providing destroyers with nuclear reactors would become cost-effective (given CBO's baseline trajectory for oil prices) only if energy use more than doubled for the entire fleet of destroyers.

The use of nuclear power has potential advantages besides savings on the cost of fuel. For example, the Navy would be less vulnerable to disruptions in the supply of oil: The alternative nuclear fleet would use about 5 million barrels of oil less per year, reducing the Navy's current annual consumption of petroleum-based fuels for aircraft and ships by about 15 percent.[5] The use of nuclear power also has some potential disadvantages, including the concerns about proliferating nuclear material that would arise if the Navy had more ships with highly enriched uranium deployed overseas. CBO, however, did not attempt to quantify those other advantages and disadvantages.

CBO's ANALYSIS AND FINDINGS

Between 2016 and 2040, the Navy plans to build 39 DDG-51 Flight III destroyers (a "flight" is a variant) and their replacements, the DDG(X) class of ship;[6] 5 LH(X) amphibious assault ships; and 12 LSD(X) amphibious dock landing ships (see Figure 1 and Box 1). CBO's main analysis compared the costs for a fleet of those 56 ships under two alternative propulsion technologies: nuclear power and conventional fuel. CBO did not consider any other class of surface ship for its analysis. Aircraft carriers are already nuclear powered, and the littoral combat ship—a relatively small high-speed ship meant for close-to-shore operations and the only other major combat ship that the Navy is planning to procure in substantial numbers over the next 30 years—is too small to accommodate a nuclear reactor. Moreover, CBO assumed that only new classes of ships would be considered candidates for nuclear systems. Thus, in constructing its hypothetical fleet, CBO assumed

The Cost-Effectiveness of Nuclear Power for Navy Surface Ships 43

that the specifications for classes of ships currently in production would not be changed, nor would existing ships be retrofitted with nuclear reactors.

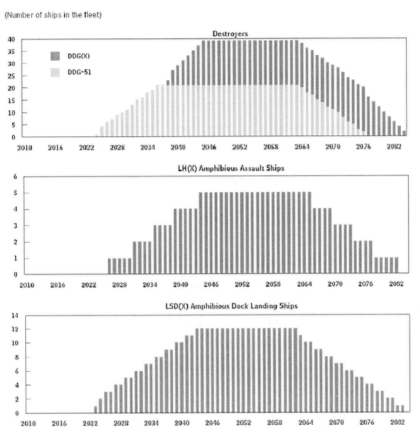

Source: Congressional Budget Office based on Department of the Navy, Report to Congress on Annual Long-Range Plan for Construction of Naval Vessels for FY 2011 (February 2010).

Note: CBO modified the Navy's shipbuilding plan slightly to accommodate the possibility of nuclear reactors, applying the same changes to the plan in evaluating both conventional and nuclear fuel alternatives. Specifically, CBO's modified plan would delay the purchase of the first DDG-51 Flight III destroyer (a "flight" is a variant) from 2016 to 2018 to allow time for integrating a nuclear reactor into that hull. CBO's modification would also replace the LHA-6 amphibious assault ship that the Navy plans to purchase in 2021 with the first hull in the LH(X) class in order to make the latter ship a candidate for nuclear power.

Figure 1. Candidate Ships for Nuclear Propulsion Systems.

Box 1. Destroyers and Amphibious Ships in the Navy's Fleet

Arleigh Burke Class Destroyer (DDG-51)

The DDG-51 Arleigh Burke class destroyers (along with the CG-47 Ticonderoga class cruisers) serve a variety of roles in the Navy's fleet. They defend aircraft carriers and amphibious ships against threats posed by other surface ships, aircraft, and submarines. Increasingly, they will provide ballistic missile defense for the fleet as well as for major theaters of operations such as Europe and Northeast Asia. They also perform many day-today missions, such as patrolling sea lanes, providing overseas presence, and conducting exercises with allies. In addition, they are capable of striking land targets with Tomahawk missiles. The Navy considers the DDG-51 class so effective that it plans to modify the design into a configuration called Flight III (ships currently under construction are called Flight IIAs), beginning in the middle part of this decade. The upgraded DDG-51 design will have a more powerful radar along with increased shipboard power and cooling capabilities and will provide a ballistic missile defense capability greater than that provided by DDG-51 Flight IIAs. The existing DDG-51s displace about 9,500 tons, but the Flight III configuration is likely to weigh more than 10,000 tons.

Wasp Class Amphibious Assault Ship (LHD)

The Navy's two types of amphibious assault ships (also known as helicopter carriers)—the LHA-1 and LHD-1—are the second-largest types of ship in the fleet (behind aircraft carriers). The new LHA-6 America class is replacing the Tarawa class LHA-1s. The first LHA-6 is still under construction and will displace about 45,000 tons. A future class of this type of ship, currently designated the LH(X), will be designed and built in the 2020s to replace the Wasp class LHDs as they retire. Amphibious assault ships form the centerpiece of amphibious ready groups and can each carry about half the troops and equipment of a Marine expeditionary unit, which is typically composed of about 2,200 marines. The ships also can carry as many as 30 helicopters and 6 fixed-wing Harrier jump jets, or up to 20 Harriers.

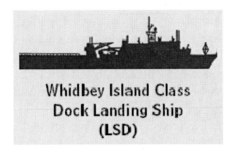

Whidbey Island Class
Dock Landing Ship
(LSD)

The Navy has four other classes of amphibious warfare ships, and such ships are divided into two types: amphibious transport docks (LPDs) and dock landing ships (LSDs). Two of those ships together provide the remaining transport capacity for a Marine expeditionary unit in an amphibious ready group. LPDs and LSDs are quite similar to each other; one major difference is that the LPDs have a hangar to embark helicopters whereas the LSDs do not, although they do have a helicopter landing area. The Navy's 12 LSDs are divided into two classes—the LSD-41 Whidbey Island and the LSD-49 Harpers Ferry—and displace 16,000 to 17,000 tons. The LSD-49 has a smaller docking well than the LSD-41 has in order to carry more troops and equipment; the LSD-41 has a larger docking well for conducting amphibious operations. The Navy plans to build one more LPD in 2012 but is not planning a direct successor to that class of ships. The service does plan to build a new class of LSDs, designated the LSD(X), beginning in 2017 to replace the existing LSDs as they retire.

The design and capabilities of the new class are unknown at this time, although the Navy's 2011 shipbuilding plan implies that they will be similar to existing LSD class ships.

Source: Congressional Budget Office.
Note: Ship silhouettes are not to scale.

CBO's analysis was also based on several assumptions about the reactors the Navy would use if it chose the nuclear power alternative and the implications of the reactors for a ship's size. CBO assumed that the Navy would design a new reactor for use in the destroyers and LSD class ships because existing reactors would not be optimally sized for those ship types. CBO further assumed that in the LH(X) amphibious assault ships, the Navy would use one of the reactors that power its aircraft carriers.[7] Yet even if the Navy outfitted the destroyers and amphibious dock landing ships with a new, smaller reactor, the use of nuclear power would require an increase of about 2,000 tons in the DDG-51's displacement, or weight (an increase of 20 percent relative to the current size of that ship), and a similar increase in the LSD(X)'s displacement (an increase of 11 percent), by CBO's estimates.[8] The LH(X), in contrast, could accommodate a nuclear reactor without any substantial increase in the ship's displacement.

In comparing life-cycle costs for the fleet of ships under the alternative propulsion systems, CBO used a present-value approach that adjusted for market risk. CBO first calculated costs over a 40-year service life for each of the 56 ships chosen for the analysis and then summarized those costs as a present value—a single amount that expresses the stream of annual costs for the ships in terms of an equivalent lump sum spent at the start of the analysis period. To arrive at that present value, CBO discounted future costs for the fleet (converted them to current dollars) using a discount rate that takes into account that money in hand now is worth more than the same amount received in the future and that the cash flows face market risk (the risk of losses that cannot be avoided by diversifying investments and for which investors require compensation). Specifically, CBO used a discount rate for the fleet's future costs equal to the estimated return that a private investor would require on a project of similar risk and duration, discounting the life-cycle costs for all ships in each class under the nuclear-fleet alternative and comparing those totals with the corresponding discounted amounts under the conventional-fleet alternative.

The results of CBO's cost-effectiveness analysis depend heavily on what happens to oil prices over the next 70 years. CBO thus calculated costs for its hypothetical fleet under a trajectory for oil prices derived from its current macroeconomic projections and also under variations of that trajectory. (For details of CBO's approach, see "The Basis for CBO's Cost Estimates" on page 9.) It also noted certain noncost factors (for example, the ability of nuclear-powered ships to operate independently of logistics ships that supply oil) that might be important but that could not be fully accounted for.

Table 1. Estimated Life-Cycle Costs for a Nuclear Versus a Conventionally Powered Fleet, Calculated as Present Values Using Risk-Adjusted Discount Rates
(Billions of 2011 dollars)

	DDG-51 and DDG(X) Destroyers		LH(X) Amphibious Assault Ships		LSD(X) Amphibious Dock Landing Ships		All Ships	
	Conventional	Nuclear	Conventional	Nuclear	Conventional	Nuclear	Conventional	Nuclear
Acquisition								
Develop a new nuclear reactora	n.a.	0.8	n.a.	0	n.a.	0.2	n.a.	1.0
Certify an additional nuclear shipyardb	n.a.	0.4	n.a.	*	n.a.	0.1	n.a.	0.5
Procure ships	36.6	55.0	6.2	8.2	6.3	11.3	49.2	74.5
Subtotal	36.6	56.2	6.2	8.2	6.3	11.6	49.2	76.0
Fuel	10.4	0	2.1	0	1.9	0	14.4	0
Personnel	19.6	24.1	4.2	4.9	4.8	6.1	28.6	35.1
Other Operations and Support	5.5	5.5	1.6	1.6	1.9	1.9	9.0	9.0
Disposal	*	0.4	*	0.1	*	0.2	*	0.7
Total	72.1	86.1	14.2	14.8	14.8	19.8	101.1	120.7

	DDG-51 and DDG(X) Destroyers		LH(X) Amphibious Assault Ships		LSD(X) Amphibious Dock Landing Ships		All Ships	
	Conventional	Nuclear	Conventional	Nuclear	Conventional	Nuclear	Conventional	Nuclear
Memorandum:								
Number of Ships Built	39	39	5	5	12	12	56	56

Source: Congressional Budget Office.

Notes: Total costs for each type of ship consist of the sum of the discounted value of the life-cycle costs for each ship of that type considered in CBO's analysis—that is, for 39 destroyers, 5 amphibious assault ships, and 12 amphibious dock landing ships. (Life-cycle costs are costs over a ship's entire 40-year service life, beginning with its acquisition and progressing through the annual expenditures over 40 years for its fuel, personnel, and other operations and support and, finally, its disposal.) Details of CBO's present-value calculations and discounting methods are discussed in the text.

A conventionally powered DDG-51 Flight III destroyer (a "flight" is a variant) is expected to have a full-load displacement (weight) of 10,000 tons; CBO assumed that a nuclear-powered DDG-51 would displace 12,000 tons. CBO also assumed that the replacement class, the DDG(X), would displace 11,000 tons if conventionally powered and 13,000 tons if nuclear powered; that the LSD(X) amphibious dock landing ship would displace 18,000 tons if conventionally powered and 20,000 tons if nuclear powered; and that the LH(X) amphibious assault ship would displace 45,000 tons in either case (the ship would have adequate capacity to accommodate nuclear reactors with no increase in displacement).

n.a. = not applicable; * = between zero and $50 million.

a   CBO allocated the total $1 billion cost to develop a new nuclear reactor equally among the 51 destroyers and LSD(X)s under the nuclear-fleet alternative. No costs were allocated to the LH(X); CBO assumed those ships would be outfitted with one of the A1B reactors that the Navy plans to use in the new Gerald R. Ford class (CVN-78) of aircraft carriers.

b   CBO allocated the total $500 million cost to certify an additional nuclear shipyard equally among all 56 ships under the nuclear-fleet alternative.

The Cost-Effectiveness of Nuclear Power for Navy Surface Ships 49

In addition, CBO compared its analysis and results with those from an earlier study conducted by the Navy to assess the advantages and disadvantages of extending nuclear power to a wider range of Navy ships.

Costs under CBO's Projected Trajectory for Oil Prices

A nuclear-powered fleet comprising the three classes of ships considered in the analysis would cost the Navy more than a conventionally powered fleet under CBO's projected trajectory for oil prices (see Table 1). According to CBO's projections, the prices that U.S. refiners pay for oil will rise from $86 per barrel in 2011 to $95 per barrel (in 2011 dollars) in 2021, and then continue to escalate at a real annual rate of 1 percent thereafter. Under that projected price path, the present-value costs in 2011 for a nuclear-powered fleet would be higher than those for a conventionally powered fleet by about $14 billion (19 percent) for destroyers, $0.6 billion (4 percent) for LH(X) amphibious assault ships, and nearly $5 billion (33 percent) for LSD(X) amphibious dock landing ships.

The main reason is that the reduction in the Navy's costs for conventional fossil fuel that the use of nuclear power would lead to would not be large enough to compensate for the increase in the acquisition costs for nuclear-powered ships. Moreover, such ships require larger and more highly trained crews than their conventional counterparts do, so their personnel costs would be greater as well. Other differences in costs between the fleets do not make up a significant percentage of total costs. (The costs for designing a new reactor for the destroyers and the LSD(X) ships, certifying a third commercial shipyard for nuclear work—discussed later—and disposing of nuclear reactors at the end of the ships' service lives would each be less than 1 percent of the nuclear fleet's total discounted costs.)

Costs under a Higher Projected Trajectory for Oil Prices

If oil prices followed the path that CBO has forecast, a nuclear fleet would be more expensive than a conventional fleet. The trajectory of oil prices, however, is highly uncertain. If the price of oil rose more rapidly over the service lives of those ships than CBO has projected, conventionally powered ships could become more expensive than nuclear-powered ships; that is, the higher cost of petroleum for conventional ships would begin to overtake the higher cost of acquisition for nuclear ships.

CBO thus considered a case in which the price of oil grows at a rate higher than the 1 percent real growth in CBO's baseline, starting from the same value of $86 per barrel in 2011. A fleet of nuclear destroyers would become cost-effective only if the real rate of growth of oil prices exceeded 3.4 percent per year over the 2012–2084 period (see Figure 2); that projected rate would imply a price for oil (in 2011 dollars) of $223 per barrel or more in 2040 and higher prices in later years. Similarly, a fleet of nuclear LH(X) amphibious assault ships would become cost-effective at an annual real growth rate for oil prices of 1.7 percent, or a price of $140 per barrel in 2040, and a fleet of nuclear LSD(X) amphibious dock landing ships would become cost-effective at a real growth rate of 4.7 percent per year, or a price of $323 per barrel. Under an assumption that the prices of goods used to build and operate ships would not systematically vary with economic conditions (meaning that the appropriate discount rate would not need to take market risk into account), the rates of growth of oil prices at which nuclear propulsion would become cost-effective would be slightly higher (see the appendix for details).

Costs with Increased Energy Use by Destroyers

Another key factor about which there is considerable uncertainty is the amount of energy that new surface ships would use during their operations—particularly ships that, like destroyers, require large amounts of energy for purposes other than propulsion. Changes in those amounts could have a substantial effect on the relative costs of nuclear and conventional power. Power use could be lower on conventional ships if the Navy used a hybrid electric drive to reduce fuel consumption. Alternatively, and probably more likely, power use could be higher because of the new ships' larger radars, new weapon systems, other electronic systems, and a possible boost in the ships' steaming hours. However, those effects on the costs of the nuclear fleet would be relatively small. For example, if the DDG(X) were to consume 50 percent more energy than the current generation of destroyers, the percentage by which the cost of a fleet of nuclear destroyers would exceed the cost of a conventional fleet would decline from 19 percent to 16 percent.[9] Using an approach similar to the one it used to assess sensitivity to oil prices, CBO estimated that providing destroyers with nuclear reactors would become cost-effective (given CBO's baseline trajectory for oil prices) only if energy use more than doubled for the entire fleet of destroyers.

The Cost-Effectiveness of Nuclear Power for Navy Surface Ships 51

Other Considerations

Some observers argue that compared with conventionally powered ships, nuclear-powered ships are a better option for the Navy even if they cost more.[10] Nuclear ships may be able to steam faster and operate a larger, more powerful radar (which, like the propulsion system, would rely on the reactor for energy); they may also be capable of operating for longer periods without restocking supplies or fuel. The extent of those potential advantages would depend on how the nuclear ships operated. On the one hand, such ships might need to restock perishable food or fuel for aircraft even if they did not require fuel for propulsion. Or nuclear ships might operate in battle groups with conventional ships and be tied to the conventional ships' operating schedules. On the other hand, nuclear-powered surface combatants might be more effective than conventional ships as escorts to nuclear carriers because the carriers would no longer be tied to the operating schedules of their escorts. CBO, however, was unable to quantify such considerations or account for them in its cost comparison.

Comparing CBO's Analysis with the Navy's Study of Nuclear Power for Future Surface Combatants

The Navy has also studied the possibility of using nuclear power in some of its future destroyers and amphibious warfare ships, the current versions of which are powered by conventional gas turbines.[11] The Navy found that for a likely range of oil prices, the costs for nuclear-powered ships would exceed the costs for equivalent ships with conventional power plants—the same conclusion that CBO reached. Unlike CBO's study, however, the Navy's analysis compared individual ships equipped with the two types of power plants without regard to the phased introduction of ships into the fleet. That is, the study did not account for the fact that even if oil prices were assumed to grow quite rapidly, the potential savings from moving to a nuclear-powered fleet would accrue largely in the future—because the new ships would require decades to be fully phased in to the fleet. Nor did the Navy's study account for the time value of money—the analysis did not compare costs calculated in terms of their present values. If it was, indeed, cost-effective to gradually shift a class of ships to nuclear power, the savings would increase as more nuclear ships were built over time. However, under CBO's present-value approach, the savings in fuel costs associated with the ships that entered the fleet in later years were heavily discounted because the savings accrued so far into the future.

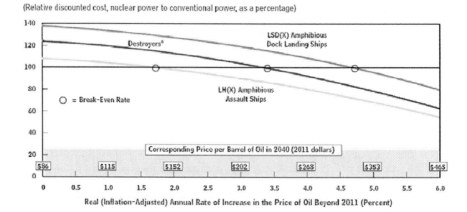

Source: Congressional Budget Office.

Notes: The break-even rate is the annual rate at which the price of oil must increase above general inflation, starting in 2011, so that life-cycle costs for ships equipped with nuclear propulsion systems equal 100 percent of the life-cycle costs for the same ships with conventional propulsion systems. CBO estimated break-even rates of 4.7 percent for LSD(X) amphibious dock landing ships, 3.4 percent for destroyers, and 1.7 percent for LH(X) amphibious assault ships.

Total costs for each type of ship consist of the sum of the discounted value of the life-cycle costs for each ship of that type considered in CBO's analysis—that is, for 12 amphibious dock landing ships, 39 destroyers, and 5 amphibious assault ships. (Life-cycle costs are costs over a ship's entire 40-year service life, beginning with its acquisition and progressing through the annual expenditures over 40 years for its fuel, personnel, and other operations and support and, finally, its disposal.) Details of CBO's discounting method and selection of rates are discussed in the text.

[a] Includes DDG-51 Flight III (a "flight" is a variant) and DDG(X) destroyers.

Figure 2. Break-Even Rates for Oil Prices at Which Life-Cycle Costs, Discounted Using Risk-Adjusted Rates, Are Equal for a Nuclear and a Conventionally Powered Fleet.

THE BASIS FOR CBO'S COST ESTIMATES

In calculating the overall costs of a fleet of new surface combatants under alternative propulsion systems, CBO used several different models to project costs over the ships' service lives. CBO began, however, with some general assumptions that were independent of how a ship was powered. First, CBO assumed that the ships chosen for its analysis would each take 5 years to build and have a service life of 40 years. Second, funds for procurement would be appropriated for the first of the new ships in 2016, although funding for research, development, testing, and evaluation would be provided sooner. Third, the first of the new ships would enter the fleet in 2023; the last of them would be procured in 2040, enter the fleet in 2045, and be retired in 2084.

CBO grouped its estimates of life-cycle costs for the new ships into the following categories:

- Acquisition and other onetime costs;
- Fuel;
- Personnel;
- Other operations and support (for example, maintenance); and
- Disposal.

In its calculations, CBO first considered costs incurred in earlier Navy shipbuilding programs that had produced ships similar to those in its hypothetical fleet. It then adjusted some of those cost elements for differences in the ships' displacement (weight). CBO used separate models to estimate acquisition costs and the different categories of operating costs (fuel, personnel, and maintenance); inputs for the models included historical operating costs and operating profiles (for example, quarterly averages of steaming hours under way and steaming hours not under way) from the Navy's Visibility and Management of Operating and Support Costs (VAMOSC) system.[12] So that expenditures made in different years and with different amounts of price risk (the risk associated with the amount of the cash outlays that the government will make in the future) could be appropriately compared, CBO expressed the total cost of the fleet under each alternative propulsion system as a present value in 2011.

Acquisition and Other Onetime Costs

CBO estimated acquisition costs for the new ships using a model that encompasses expenditures for research, design, and engineering as well as for actual construction. The model takes into account the effects of learning (unit costs—the costs of each ship constructed—decline as more ships of the same class are built in a continuous production run over a period of time) and production rates (unit costs are reduced when multiple ships of the same class are built concurrently in the same shipyard).

The model also reflects CBO's expectation that the costs of labor and materials in the naval shipbuilding industry will rise more rapidly than will general inflation during the first 35 years of the analysis—the period during which all of the ships that CBO considered would be authorized and funding would be provided by the Congress.[13] In particular, CBO projects that the composite growth of shipbuilding costs will outpace inflation (as measured by the gross domestic product price index) by an average of 1.9 percentage points per year between 2011 and 2017 and by about 1.5 percentage points per year from 2018 through 2045. (Although CBO's analysis considered operating and disposal costs for ships during a period that extended to 2084, shipbuilding inflation is germane only through 2045—because all of the ships would be built by then.) Thus, in CBO's estimation, a ship costing $2.5 billion to build in 2011, for example, would cost $3.4 billion (in 2011 dollars) to build in 2030.[14]

Additional Acquisition Costs for Nuclear-Powered Ships
The Navy could apply different solutions to providing the three classes of new ships with nuclear propulsion systems, but for its analysis, CBO assumed the following:

- The Navy would use one of the twin A1B reactors that will power the new Ford class (CVN-78) of nuclear aircraft carriers to power the LH(X) amphibious assault ships, and
- The Navy would design a new reactor—smaller than the A1B reactor but larger than the reactor in the Virginia class submarines—for the destroyers and LSD(X) amphibious dock landing ships. That activity would entail a onetime cost of about $1 billion, by the Navy's estimates.[15]

In CBO's estimation, the acquisition-cost premium for a nuclear versus a conventional ship would average about $1 billion per hull, but it would vary by the class of ship. The initial fuel core for a modern reactor lasts for the life of the ship, and the U.S. government already owns enough nuclear material to supply all of the ships considered in this analysis. Moreover, unlike the case with aircraft carriers, which the Navy expects to serve in the fleet for 50 years, the ships that CBO considered would require no additional outlays for midlife refueling. Thus, CBO estimated that the acquisition-cost premium for a nuclear ship would be about $1.1 billion per destroyer, $0.8 billion per LSD(X), and $0.9 billion per LH(X); those amounts represent some additional expenditures for nuclear fuel together with the cost of the nuclear reactor and its cooling and other support systems, and the associated greater displacement of the destroyers and LSD(X) ships if they are nuclear powered.

The Navy has not built nuclear-powered surface ships for several decades but has substantial experience in procuring and operating other types of nuclear-powered ships. Therefore, the costs for nuclear ships should be no less certain than those for conventional ships. The engine technologies for both are "mature." The technology likely to be used for the new ships if conventional propulsion systems are chosen—the General Electric LM2500 gas turbine, a derivative of the General Electric TF39 aircraft engine—has been used on the Navy's Spruance class destroyers (first commissioned in September 1975) and Oliver Hazard Perry class frigates (first commissioned in December 1977). In addition, the Navy has over 50 years of experience in building a series of ever-evolving nuclear propulsion systems.[16]

Any difficulties associated with outfitting a new class of ships with nuclear propulsion would probably be limited to the lead ship of a class. The costs of a lead ship are notoriously difficult to predict because many of the problems that arise during production of a new class or flight (variant) of vessels are resolved during construction of that ship; in many cases, costs drop precipitously for the second ship of a class or flight and then generally follow a smooth, gradual downward curve for the duration of the production run. CBO did not attempt to quantify or account for the unpredictability of the cost of the lead ships. Rather, because nuclear fuel is already available in sufficient quantity, CBO treated the price of oil—a commodity that cannot be fully stockpiled in advance—as the only significant source of uncertainty in the cost of propulsion systems for the ships in this analysis. (However, CBO's analysis also incorporated uncertainty in the cost of building the nonpropulsion parts of the ships, as discussed below.)

Additional Onetime Costs for a Nuclear-Powered Fleet

Building nuclear-powered ships for CBO's hypothetical fleet might require an additional shipyard to be certified for nuclear construction. Two commercial shipyards are currently certified to build nuclear-powered ships: General Dynamics Electric Boat (which has traditionally built nuclear submarines but not surface ships) and Newport News Shipyard. The Navy plans to build the 56 ships considered in this analysis in any case. The question is whether the two shipyards could handle the workload involved in building 56 nuclear destroyers and amphibious warfare ships over the next 30 years in addition to the construction of carriers and submarines that the Navy is planning. Simple arithmetic implies that an average of about two new ships would begin construction each year, but each ship would remain under construction for about six years. During the peak shipbuilding years, as many as 18 of the 56 ships might be in one stage of construction or another.

The two shipyards that traditionally build conventional destroyers—General Dynamics Bath Iron Works and Ingalls Shipyard—have the capacity to build that many ships in a year. Just a few years ago, Bath Iron Works had 8 destroyers in various stages of construction, and Ingalls Shipyard had 10 ships (including 2 commercial vessels) in progress. The trend in the shipyards is toward building ships on land in so-called super- or megamodules, which require considerably less pier space (a rate-limiting factor) for much of the construction period.[17] Further, the shipyards have the capacity to handle even more ships than the statistics cited above; even if pier space or other aspects of the shipyards' physical plants had to be increased, the costs of doing so would be small relative to the procurement and operating costs that dominate this analysis. Another factor in such construction is the amount of labor required. To build more ships, the shipyards also might have to increase their workforces. CBO included the recurring costs of employing those workers in its estimates of procurement costs but not any onetime costs to recruit and train additional workers. Again, however, those costs would be small in the context of procurement and operating costs for the ships.

Although the two existing nuclear-certified shipyards may have sufficient capacity to build the 56 ships in CBO's hypothetical fleet, the Navy might choose instead to certify one of the other commercial shipyards, such as Bath Iron Works or the Ingalls Shipyard, for nuclear work. The shipyard not selected for certification could still build modules that would be integrated into ships at one of the certified shipyards. For example, if Bath Iron Works was certified for nuclear work, the Navy might contract with the Ingalls Shipyard to build one-third of a ship while Bath built the other two-thirds—not unlike the contract arrangement used for the DDG-1000 destroyer program today. Or the arrangement could be reversed, with Ingalls certified as the nuclear shipyard.[18] CBO assumed for its analysis that the Navy would certify one additional shipyard at an estimated cost of about $500 million.[19]

Costs for Other Supporting Infrastructure and Logistics

The Navy's existing shore infrastructure, including maintenance and repair facilities, currently supports nuclear-powered aircraft carriers and submarines. CBO assumed that it would be sufficient to accommodate the additional nuclear ships that would be built under the nuclear-fleet alternative and did not include any additional infrastructure costs for support of the 56 new ships.

CBO estimated that, on balance, the Navy's need for combat logistics ships—which resupply other ships with fuel for use by the ships themselves and by naval aircraft, and with ammunition, food, and other supplies—would be about the same whether or not the Navy switched to nuclear power for its new surface combatants. If the Navy made that shift, deliveries of petroleum-based fuel at sea would decline only slowly because the fleets of destroyers, LH(X) ships, and LSD(X) ships would not become all-nuclear until the 2040s. In the meantime, the Navy plans to build 53 (conventionally powered) littoral combat ships in addition to the two that have already been completed, and all of those ships would continue to require fuel to be delivered at sea. CBO further assumed that, compared with what was required for conventional ships, nuclear ships would require the same degree of restocking of commodities, other than ships' fuel; nuclear ships might even require greater amounts of those stores, in view of the larger crews that CBO expects would be needed aboard the nuclear-powered ships (discussed below).

Fuel

CBO estimated rates of fuel consumption for conventionally powered ships in its hypothetical fleet by using historical data for selected Navy surface ships. Such ships consume fuel while they are under way and, to a lesser extent, while they are not under way. (For example, fuel may be converted to electricity to provide such services as lighting and climate control while a ship is in port.) Where necessary, CBO adjusted underway fuel consumption to reflect differences in displacement between the ships in the hypothetical new fleet and the ships selected as historical antecedents.

In general, a larger ship consumes more fuel than a smaller one and thus offers a greater opportunity to save money by replacing conventional engines with nuclear reactors. Yet how much fuel a ship consumes depends not only on the ship's size but also on the design of its hull and its mission (for example, the distances it is expected to travel during a typical deployment and the size of the radar and other electronics). For example, the DDG-51 Flight III destroyer is the smallest ship that CBO considered in this analysis—the destroyer displaces (weighs) 10,000 tons as opposed to the LSD(X), which displaces 18,000 tons, and the LH(X), which displaces 45,000 tons. But the destroyer consumes more fuel per ton per hour when under way than do the larger ships. Thus, replacing the destroyer's conventional power plant with a nuclear reactor would become cost-effective under a lower projected trajectory for oil prices than would be the case for the somewhat larger LSD(X).

Oil prices have been volatile over the past few decades and are difficult to predict (see Box 2). After peaking at almost $130 per barrel in June and July 2008, they had plummeted by December 2008 to about $36 per barrel; they then began to grow again and by March 2011 exceeded $100 per barrel.[20] CBO's macroeconomic projections as of January 2011 show oil prices rising to $95 per barrel (in 2011 dollars) by 2021.[21] Thereafter, CBO assumed, prices would escalate at a real annual rate of 1 percent. CBO also considered other trajectories for the price of oil to estimate the break-even rate of growth that would render the two types of propulsion systems equally costly.

The cost of the fuel delivered to Navy ships comprises many elements besides the price of crude oil. CBO thus used a method developed by the Navy for calculating a "fully burdened" cost of fuel—one that includes the price of crude oil refining, delivery of the fuel using the Navy's supply ships, necessary shore facilities, and administrative services through the Department of Defense's supply system. Extrapolating from the Navy's calculations, CBO projected the fully burdened cost of fuel (which comprises both a fixed- and a variable-cost component) on the basis of its historical relationship to the price of crude oil. For example, a price of $86 per barrel of crude oil would imply a fully burdened cost of $178 per barrel—or a burden rate of 107 percent.[22] If oil prices followed CBO's projected trajectory—increasing to $95 per barrel in 2021 and then continuing to escalate at a real rate of 1 percent per year—prices would reach $114 per barrel by 2040 (in 2011 dollars). By extension, the burdened price in 2040 would be $222, and the burden rate would be 95 percent.

Personnel

CBO also applied the notion of fully burdened costs to its estimates of expenditures on military personnel for the hypothetical fleet; in that case, its calculations encompassed basic military pay, withholding taxes paid by the federal government, housing benefits, current and future health benefits, retirement benefits, tax advantages, and veterans' benefits.[23] CBO estimated the costs in each category using data from 2010 and then projected the growth in each using rates consistent with its long-term economic projections (overall real growth of about 1 percent per year).[24] For nuclear-powered ships, CBO adjusted personnel costs in two ways: It increased basic military pay by 10 percent to reflect the mix of higher-level skills appropriate to a nuclear vessel, and it added 35 crew members to each ship's complement to support the operation of the reactor.

Other Operations and Support

CBO estimated average maintenance costs for the three kinds of ships by using historical data for similar ship classes and then adjusting those data for the differences in the ships' displacement. CBO's estimates allowed for overhauls and other periods when the ships might be unavailable because of maintenance—that is, periods when they would spend a minimal number of hours under way.

Disposal

CBO modeled disposal costs for conventional ships as a function of their displacement; for example, it would cost about $1 million to dispose of a conventional destroyer but about $9 million to dispose of the much larger LH(X) amphibious ship. For nuclear-powered ships, CBO estimated, on the basis of data provided by the Navy, that it would cost an additional $140 million to dispose of a single reactor from a nuclear-powered ship of any of the types considered in this analysis.[25]

COMPARING THE COSTS OF ALTERNATIVE PROPULSION SYSTEMS USING PRESENT-VALUE CALCULATIONS

The total estimated costs for CBO's hypothetical fleet under both the conventional and nuclear power alternatives depend on the estimated future costs for building and operating the ships in the fleet and the discount rates used to convert those costs to present values—a standard method for valuing an extended stream of future cash flows. CBO thus estimated projected future costs in terms of 2011 dollars; it also used risk-adjusted discount rates that attach a market price to the risk associated with the amount of the cash outlays that the government will make in the future. That "fair-value" approach measures what a private entity in a competitive market would need to be paid to voluntarily assume the costs and risks that the government is assuming on behalf of taxpayers. Such an approach provides a more complete measure of the economic cost associated with the two alternatives than does a calculation that treats the government's capacity to bear market risk as having no cost. Although the government can borrow at rates that include no extra compensation for bearing market risk, its ability to do so depends on taxpayers—who back the debt and thus bear that risk.[26]

Box 2. Fluctuating Oil Prices

In comparisons of the cost-effectiveness of using conventional versus nuclear propulsion for the Navy's planned fleet of new surface combatants, an important consideration is the future price of oil. The Congressional Budget Office (CBO) regularly projects oil prices over a 10-year period as part of the macroeconomic forecast that underlies its baseline budget projections.[1] However, for its analysis of conventional versus nuclear propulsion, CBO had to consider the trajectory of oil prices over a much longer period—a total span of 75 years, with the Navy's new surface ships expected to be built over the next 35 years and then operated for 40 more years. Such a long forecasting horizon increases the uncertainty inherent in projections of oil prices.

Oil prices can be volatile even over short periods; in recent years, they have fluctuated widely. For example, the average price of all crude oil delivered to U.S. refiners generally declined throughout the 1990s (albeit with some variability) to about $12 per barrel (in 2011 dollars) in December 1998. It then rose to $38 in September 2001; fell again to $19 per barrel in December 2001; and subsequently, from that point to the middle of 2008, increased nearly sevenfold, peaking at almost $130 per barrel in June and July of that year (see the figure to the right).[2] The average price then fell to $36 per barrel in December 2008 and began to climb again, reaching a monthly average of more than $100 per barrel in March 2011.[3] Over longer periods, the real (inflation-adjusted) price of oil has generally increased: The real price was higher in the decade that began in 2001 than in the preceding decade.

The primary reason for short-term fluctuations in oil prices is that the quantity of oil supplied and the quantity demanded are generally not very responsive to short-lived price pressures. That means that, in the face of an unexpected shortage or surplus of oil, prices may move sharply up or down in order to rebalance supply and demand in the world market. For example, the total supply of oil is strongly influenced by the nations that make up the Organization of Petroleum Exporting Countries, or OPEC.[4] OPEC controls essentially all of the spare oil production capacity in the world; if it decides to curtail its members' output, the nations outside of OPEC are seldom able to boost production in the short run to alleviate the shortage. Moreover, if prices rise rapidly, it takes time for industry and consumers to significantly lessen their demand. For example, the transportation sector accounts for about 75 percent of all petroleum consumed in the United States, and drivers (including commercial truckers) are reluctant or unable to quickly reduce the number of miles they drive.[5] In the longer run, the demand for oil in the transportation sector is more responsive to oil prices because businesses can change the way they transport their goods (for example, they can ship fewer goods by air), and consumers can choose more fuel-efficient vehicles or modify their commuting patterns.

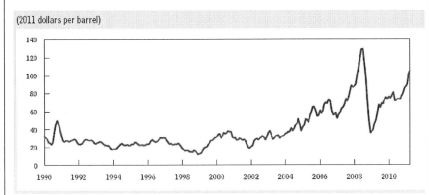

Source: Congressional Budget Office based on data from Department of Energy, Energy Information Administration, "Petroleum and Other Liquids" (www.eia.doe.gov/dnav/pet/pet_pri_rac2_dcu_nus_m.htm).

Monthly Average Price for All Oil Imported and Delivered to U.S. Refiners.

CBO bases its 10-year forecasts of oil prices partly on transactions in the futures market for oil (a market for commitments to deliver oil in the future), which reflects the developments that investors expect in the worldwide supply of and demand for oil.[6] In CBO's most recent forecast, oil prices after 2013 grow at a rate about 1 percentage point higher than that for inflation through 2021. CBO assumed for this study that the same trend would continue through 2084.[7]

That projection of long-term price growth is consistent with an outlook in which the world economy continues to expand and the increasing growth in the global demand for crude oil is satisfied by generally harder-to-access and higher-cost supplies. But oil market trends are uncertain. The rate of growth of oil prices that CBO has forecast—1 percentage point above inflation—might be lower if world demand grew more slowly than projected or if new oil reserves were discovered. Alternatively, real prices could rise faster if the growth in worldwide demand was greater than expected or if producers had more difficulty keeping pace with that growth. The policies and stability of OPEC will also influence future prices and are difficult to predict.

1. For CBO's most recent economic projections, see Congressional Budget Office, *The Budget and Economic Outlook: Fiscal Years 2011 to 2021* (January 2011).

2. The average price of all oil imported and delivered to U.S. refiners is the measure of oil prices that is calculated by the Energy Information Administration, the Department of Energy's statistical agency (see www.eia.doe.gov/dnav/pet/pet_pri_rac2_dcu_nus_m.htm), and used by CBO in its macroeconomic forecast.

3. West Texas Intermediate crude oil, which is another benchmark for oil prices, peaked at a daily price of about $145 per barrel in July 2008 and, after declining from that high point, had by the end of April 2011 again risen to more than $110 per barrel. (West Texas Intermediate is a high-quality light sweet crude oil produced in North America.) See Department of Energy, Energy Information Administration, "Petroleum and Other Liquids" (May 2, 2011; www.eia.doe.gov/dnav/pet/hist/LeafHandler.ashx?n=PET&s=RWTC&f=D).

4. For additional information on the factors that influence oil prices, see Department of Energy, Energy Information Administration, *Oil Prices and Outlook* (updated December 17, 2010; www.eia.gov/energyexplained/index.cfm?page=oil_prices).

5. See Congressional Budget Office, *Effects of Gasoline Prices on Driving Behavior and Vehicle Markets* (January 2008).

6. For a specific discussion about projecting oil prices using data from futures markets, see Congressional Budget Office, *The Budget and Economic Outlook: Fiscal Years 2006 to 2015* (January 2005).

7. To reflect the uncertainty in that projected trajectory for oil prices, CBO conducted a sensitivity analysis to determine how much faster the price of oil would have to rise to overturn the conclusion of the main analysis that conventionally powered ships are more cost-effective than nuclear-powered ships. (See "Costs Under a Higher Projected Trajectory for Oil Prices" on page 7.) As a point of comparison, the Department of Energy's Energy Information Administration (EIA) publishes 25-year projections of oil prices. (For its most recent estimates, through 2035, see "Annual Energy Outlook—2011: Reference Case Tables," April 26, 2011; www.eia.gov/forecasts/aeo/tables_ref.cfm.) As of January 2011, CBO's and EIA's projections of long-term growth in prices were similar; however, EIA projected higher rates of growth than CBO did for years up to and including 2021, whereas for years after 2021, EIA projected lower rates of growth, relative to CBO's estimates.

Under the fair-value approach, CBO used discount rates for the federal government's estimated future costs that took into account that the prices of the inputs used to build and operate ships—such as steel, labor, and fuel—would vary with economic conditions. Like the stock market, the prices of those inputs tend to be procyclical: That is, they move with the business cycle and are higher when the economy is strong and lower when the economy is weak. The positive relationship between the prices of inputs for ships and the stock market means that those prices are more likely to be high when economic resources (for example, the revenues of private firms) are relatively plentiful and low when such resources are relatively scarce. If input prices tended to be higher when economic resources were scarce, then an adjustment for market risk would increase the discounted costs. However, because input prices tend to be lower when economic conditions are generally worse and savings on such inputs are particularly valuable, an adjustment for market risk lowers the discounted costs of building and operating ships. That is, risk-adjusted discount rates are higher than the rates on Treasury securities, so the present value of the costs is lower than if no adjustment for market risk had been made.

CBO used a real discount rate of 4 percent in computing the present value of construction and operating costs other than those for fuel under the two propulsion alternatives. The rate has two components: a short-term rate of 2 percent (CBO's estimate of the real rate on short-term Treasury securities) and a "risk premium" of 2 percent.[27] CBO's choice of rates was based in part on an analysis of the historical cost of capital for the U.S. maritime industry. The rate also reflects a slight downward adjustment to account for the weaker correlation with the business cycle of the Navy's purchases of ships and ship support services—weaker, that is, than the business cycle's correlation with the overall activity of the maritime industry.

Similarly, CBO based the discount rate that it applied to future purchases of oil on its estimate of the rate of return that private-sector investors would require for holding stocks in oil companies. Although the price of oil, like that of other inputs, tends to increase with the strength of the overall economy, the relationship historically has been significantly weaker than the ties between the economy's robustness and the costs associated with building and operating ships. CBO thus used a discount rate of 3 percent for future oil purchases; the rate combines a short-term real rate of 2 percent and a risk premium of 1 percent. In determining that risk premium, CBO used information on the prices of oil futures contracts and forecasts of future oil prices, and analyzed historical data on the correlation of oil prices with market risk.[28]

To determine whether the results of its analysis were sensitive to the choice of discount rates, CBO also compared the life-cycle costs for nuclear-powered and conventionally powered fleets using a real long-term discount rate of 3 percent for all cash flows (see the appendix). That rate corresponds to CBO's projection of the real rate of return on 30-year Treasury bonds. (Coincidentally, it is also identical to CBO's estimate of the required return on investments in oil.)[29] In that case, too, the costs for a fleet of conventionally powered ships would be significantly lower than the costs for a fleet of nuclear-powered ships.

APPENDIX: SUPPLEMENTARY CALCULATIONS USING AN ALTERNATIVE DISCOUNT RATE

In its main analysis comparing the cost-effectiveness of using nuclear versus conventional power for the Navy's planned fleet of new surface ships, the Congressional Budget Office (CBO) calculated the costs for all the ships as a present value—a single amount that expressed the stream of the ships' annual costs in terms of an equivalent lump sum spent at the start of the analysis period. In those calculations, future costs were "discounted" (converted into current dollars) using a rate that took into account two factors: Money in hand is worth more than the same amount received in the future, and the cash flows face market risk. (Market risk is the risk of losses that investors cannot avoid by diversifying holdings and for which they require some compensation.) In particular, CBO used discount rates for future financial costs equal to the estimated return that a private investor would require on a project of similar risk and duration: a real (inflation-adjusted) discount rate of 3 percent in computing the present value of conventional fuel costs and a real discount rate of 4 percent in calculating construction and operating costs (for both nuclear and conventional ships) other than those for fuel.

In an alternative analysis, CBO recalculated the cost comparison using Treasury rates for discounting—specifically, using a real discount rate of 3 percent for all categories of costs. That rate is based on CBO's forecast of the rates of return on long-term (30-year) Treasury bonds; that it is identical to the discount rate CBO used to compute the present value of conventional fuel costs in the main analysis is coincidental. (CBO determined the discount rates for its main analysis by entirely different methods, as discussed in "Comparing the Costs of Alternative Propulsion Systems Using Present-Value Calculations" on page 13.) This alternative calculation does not take the cost of market risk into account; rather, it reflects the compensation that investors would require to make long-term investments that they believe entail no risk of loss from defaults. It also reflects the method of discounting (and, over the past decade, the approximate discount rate) used by executive branch agencies.[1]

Using the same rate (3 percent) to discount all costs— rather than applying a lower adjustment for risk (that is, a lower discount rate) to fuel costs than to other types of costs, as in the main analysis—leads to different estimates of the comparative cost-effectiveness of nuclear versus conventional power but the same net result: Nuclear ships would be more expensive unless oil prices sustained rapid growth through 2084. Under the alternative approach of discounting all costs at 3 percent, nuclear power would be even more expensive than conventional power relative to the findings from the main analysis, because the fuel savings would no longer be discounted at a rate lower than that used for other costs. As a corollary, the price of oil would have to grow more rapidly than in the trajectory presented in the main text before the costs for conventional fuel began to overtake the higher acquisition costs associated with nuclear-powered ships, thus making the use of nuclear propulsion cost-effective.

CBO assumed for this alternative analysis that the price of oil would follow the same projected trajectory that CBO used for the main analysis: Oil prices start at $86 per barrel in 2011 and grow at a rate about 1 percentage point per year above that of general inflation. In CBO's estimation, the present-value costs in 2011, if calculated using Treasury rates for discounting, for a nuclear-powered fleet relative to a conventionally powered one would be about $20 billion (22 percent) higher for destroyers, $1.4 billion (8 percent) higher for LH(X) amphibious assault ships, and $6.6 billion (35 percent) higher for LSD(X) amphibious dock landing ships (see Table A-1). For the sake of comparison, the findings from CBO's main analysis, which used risk-adjusted discount rates, were that costs would be higher for a nuclear-powered fleet by about $14 billion (or 19 percent) for destroyers, by $0.6 billion (4 percent) for LH(X) amphibious assault ships, and by nearly $5 billion (33 percent) for LSD(X) amphibious dock landing ships. The costs for conventional fuel that are avoided by the use of nuclear power—costs that are now, in this alternative analysis, discounted at the same rate as other costs and thus relatively smaller—would not be large enough to compensate for the increased acquisition costs of nuclear-powered ships.

In addition to the case just described, CBO also considered one in which the price of oil again starts from the value of $86 per barrel in 2011 but then increases over time at a fixed rate that exceeds the rate of general inflation by some amount greater than 1 percentage point. In CBO's estimation, a fleet of nuclear destroyers would become cost-effective under such a price path (and the alternative discount rate assumption) if the real annual rate of growth in oil prices exceeded 3.9 percent (see Figure A-1). Such a scenario implies a price for oil of $260 or more per barrel (in 2011 dollars) in 2040. Similarly, a fleet of nuclear-powered LH(X) amphibious assault ships would become cost-effective at a real annual growth rate for oil prices of 2.5 percent (for a price of $173 per barrel in 2040); and a fleet of nuclear-powered LSD(X) amphibious dock landing ships would become cost-effective if the price of oil grew at a real annual rate of 5.2 percent (for a price of $373 per barrel in 2040). The comparable findings from CBO's main analysis are a real annual rate of growth in oil prices of 3.4 percent and an implied price of $223 per barrel for destroyers, growth of 1.7 percent and an implied price of $140 per barrel for LH(X) amphibious assault ships, and growth of 4.7 percent and an implied price of $323 per barrel for amphibious dock landing ships.

Table A-1. Estimated Life-Cycle Costs for a Nuclear Versus a Conventionally Powered Fleet, Calculated as Present Values Using Treasury Rates for Discounting
(Billions of 2011 dollars)

	DDG-51 and DDG(X) Destroyers		LH(X) Amphibious Assault Ships		LSD(X) Amphibious Dock Landing Ships		All Ships	
	Conventional	Nuclear	Conventional	Nuclear	Conventional	Nuclear	Conventional	Nuclear
Acquisition								
Develop a new nuclear reactora	n.a.	0.8	n.a.	0	n.a.	0.2	n.a.	1.0
Certify an additional nuclear shipyardb	n.a.	0.4	n.a.	*	n.a.	0.1	n.a.	0.5
Procure ships	44.9	67.2	7.5	9.8	7.4	13.3	59.8	90.4
Subtotal	44.9	68.4	7.5	9.8	7.4	13.6	59.8	91.9
Fuel	10.4	0	2.1	0	1.9	0	14.4	0
Personnel	28.2	34.7	6.2	7.2	6.9	8.8	41.3	50.8
Other Operations and Support	7.9	7.9	2.4	2.4	2.7	2.7	13.0	13.0
Disposal	*	0.8	*	0.1	*	0.3	*	1.2
Total	91.4	111.8	18.2	19.6	18.8	25.4	128.5	156.9

	DDG-51 and DDG(X) Destroyers		LH(X) Amphibious Assault Ships		LSD(X) Amphibious Dock Landing Ships		All Ships	
	Conventional	Nuclear	Conventional	Nuclear	Conventional	Nuclear	Conventional	Nuclear
Memorandum:								
Number of Ships Built	39	39	5	5	12	12	56	56

Source: Congressional Budget Office.

Notes: Total costs for each type of ship consist of the sum of the discounted value of the life-cycle costs for each ship of that type considered in CBO's analysis—that is, for 39 destroyers, 5 amphibious assault ships, and 12 amphibious dock landing ships. (Life-cycle costs are costs over a ship's entire 40-year service life, beginning with its acquisition and progressing through the annual expenditures over 40 years for its fuel, personnel, and other operations and support and, finally, its disposal.) Details of CBO's present-value calculations and discounting methods are discussed in the text.

A conventionally powered DDG-51 Flight III destroyer (a "flight" is a variant) is expected to have a full-load displacement (weight) of 10,000 tons; CBO assumed that a nuclear-powered DDG-51 would displace 12,000 tons. CBO also assumed that the replacement class, the DDG(X), would displace 11,000 tons if conventionally powered and 13,000 tons if nuclear powered; that the LSD(X) amphibious dock landing ship would displace 18,000 tons if conventionally powered and 20,000 tons if nuclear powered; and that the LH(X) amphibious assault ship would displace 45,000 tons in either case (the ship would have adequate capacity to accommodate nuclear reactors with no increase in displacement).

n.a. = not applicable; * = between zero and $50 million.

a   CBO allocated the total $1 billion cost to develop a new nuclear reactor equally among the 51 destroyers and LSD(X)s under the nuclear-fleet alternative. No costs were allocated to the LH(X); CBO assumed those ships would be outfitted with one of the A1B reactors that the Navy plans to use in the new Gerald R. Ford class (CVN-78) of aircraft carriers.

b   CBO allocated the total $500 million cost to certify an additional nuclear shipyard equally among all 56 ships under the nuclear-fleet alternative.

The Cost-Effectiveness of Nuclear Power for Navy Surface Ships

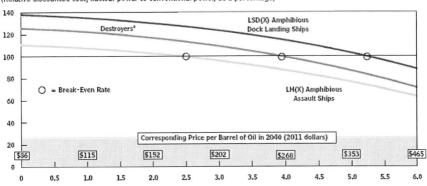

Source: Congressional Budget Office.

Notes: The break-even rate is the annual rate at which the price of oil must increase above general inflation, starting in 2011, so that life-cycle costs for ships equipped with nuclear propulsion systems equal 100 percent of the life-cycle costs for the same ships with conventional propulsion systems. CBO estimated break-even rates of 5.2 percent for LSD(X) amphibious dock landing ships, 3.9 percent for destroyers, and 2.5 percent for LH(X) amphibious assault ships.

Total costs for each type of ship consist of the sum of the discounted value of the life-cycle costs for each ship of that type considered in CBO's analysis—that is, for 12 amphibious dock landing ships, 39 destroyers, and 5 amphibious assault ships. (Life-cycle costs are costs over a ship's entire 40-year service life, beginning with its acquisition and progressing through the annual expenditures over 40 years for its fuel, personnel, and other operations and support and, finally, its disposal.) Details of CBO's discounting method and selection of rates are discussed in the text.

[a.] Includes DDG-51 Flight III (a "flight" is a variant) and DDG(X) destroyers.

Figure A-1. Break-Even Rates for Oil Prices at Which Life-Cycle Costs, Discounted Using Treasury Rates, Are Equal for a Nuclear and a Conventionally Powered Fleet.

End Notes

[1] For details of that plan, see Department of the Navy, Report to Congress on Annual Long-Range Plan for Construction of Naval Vessels for FY 2011 (February 2010); see also Congressional Budget Office, An Analysis of the Navy's Fiscal Year 2011 Shipbuilding Plan (May 2010).

[2] For CBO's most recent economic projections, see Congressional Budget Office, The Budget and Economic Outlook: Fiscal Years 2011 to 2021 (January 2011).

[3] Oil prices in the first four months of 2011 have averaged about $10 per barrel more than in CBO's January forecast for this year and could be higher or lower over the rest of the year. CBO expects to update its macroeconomic forecast in August.

[4] CBO forecasts oil prices in part on the basis of futures markets in oil. For a discussion of that approach, see Congressional Budget Office, The Budget and Economic Outlook: Fiscal Years 2006 to 2015 (January 2005).

[5] Those fuel-reduction findings are based on CBO's analysis and on data provided to CBO by the Defense Logistics Agency in April 2011. See also Ronald O'Rourke, Navy Ship Propulsion Technologies: Options for Reducing Oil Use—Background for Congress, Report for Congress RL33360 (Congressional Research Service, January 26, 2007).

[6] The DDG-51 Flight III destroyer would, among other changes, incorporate the new Air and Missile Defense Radar that is now under development. The new radar is larger and more powerful than the radars on the earlier DDG-51s.

[7] Each of the Navy's current aircraft carriers (with the exception of U.S.S. Enterprise) uses two nuclear reactors of a design known as the A4W. The Navy's newest aircraft carrier, U.S.S. Gerald R. Ford, will also use two reactors of a new design, designated the A1B. An LH(X) amphibious ship, which is slightly less than half the size of a nuclear-powered aircraft carrier, could accommodate one of the A1B reactors to be used in the Gerald R. Ford. However, outfitting a destroyer or an LSD(X) amphibious ship with an A1B-sized reactor would require a significant increase in the size of those ships to accommodate the reactor and its cooling and other support systems. Nor could those ships be outfitted with the nuclear reactors that the Navy currently installs in its Virginia class submarines, because those reactors would be too small to adequately power a destroyer or an LSD(X). CBO assumed that the Navy would instead design a new reactor for its destroyers and LSD(X) ships.

[8] Navy officials, in a personal communication in April 2011, provided CBO with an estimate of 3,000 tons for the increase in the displacement of the DDG-51 or the LSD that would be necessary to accommodate a nuclear reactor. However, CBO estimates, on the basis of other data provided by the Navy and various projected changes in design, that a new reactor would require an increase of only 2,000 tons in the ships' displacement. The use of existing reactors would require a greater increase in size, which in turn would boost the fleet's total costs more than would the design of a new reactor. In other words, if the Navy was going to put a nuclear reactor on its new destroyers and amphibious dock landing ships, designing a new reactor, by CBO's estimates, would be more cost-effective than using an existing reactor.

[9] In April 2011, the Navy indicated to CBO that power use by the DDG(X) might be 50 percent greater, according to preliminary analyses, than would have been projected on the basis of historical antecedents, in part because of additional missile defense missions. If the use of power by the DDG-51 Flight III ships matched CBO's projections and power use for the follow-on DDG(X) class was 50 percent greater than that for the current DDG-51s, the effect on the discounted present value of costs would be small— because the DDG(X) would constitute only part of the destroyer fleet, because CBO's estimates already account for some growth in energy use, and because DDG(X) operations would occur further in the future and receive relatively less weight in the estimates.

[10] For a summary of some of those arguments—though not an endorsement of them—see Hans M. Kristensen, William M. Arkin, and Joshua Handler, Aircraft Carriers: The Limits of Nuclear Power, Neptune Papers No. 7 (June 1994); and Government Accounting Office,

Nuclear or Conventional Power for Surface Combatant Ships? PSAD 77-74 (March 21, 1977).

[11] Section 130 of the Fiscal Year 2006 National Defense Authorization Act (Public Law 109-163) directed the Navy to examine the effectiveness of applying nuclear power to surface combatants (cruisers and destroyers) and amphibious warfare ships. For the Navy's response, see Naval Sea Systems Command, Report to Congress on Alternative Propulsion Methods for Surface Combatants and Amphibious Warfare Ships (January 2007).

[12] The Navy's VAMOSC management information system (www.ncca.navy.mil/services collects and reports on historical operating and support costs and related information for the Navy's and the Marine Corps' weapon systems.

[13] See Congressional Budget Office, An Analysis of the Navy's Fiscal Year 2011 Shipbuilding Plan, pp. 12–13.

[14] CBO does not expect shipbuilding costs to continue forever to grow at a faster rate than the costs of goods and services in the economy as a whole; if that were to happen, the price of ships would eventually outstrip the Navy's ability to pay for them, even in very small numbers.

[15] The Navy provided CBO with data on design costs in February 2009. CBO adjusted those data and divided the $1 billion cost equally among each of the destroyers and LSD(X)s in the hypothetical fleet. It allocated no additional design costs to the LH(X)s.

[16] The Navy commissioned its first nuclear-powered submarine, U.S.S. Nautilus (SSN-571), in September 1954; that boat went to sea for the first time in January 1955. The Navy commissioned its first nuclear-powered surface ships, the cruiser U.S.S. Long Beach (CGN-9) and the aircraft carrier U.S.S. Enterprise (CVN-65), in September 1961 and November 1961, respectively. For additional details, see Ronald O'Rourke, Navy Nuclear-Powered Surface Ships: Background, Issues, and Options for Congress, Report for Congress RL33946 (Congressional Research Service, June 10, 2010).

[17] The Navy notes that, rather than saving pier space, the primary benefit of modular construction is efficiency.

[18] The Ingalls Shipyard has some experience with nuclear-powered vessels, having built 12 nuclear submarines, the last one being the U.S.S. Parche (SSN-683), which was procured in 1968 and entered service in 1974. In addition, Ingalls has overhauled or refueled 11 nuclear-powered submarines. However, the Ingalls' nuclear-certified facility was decommissioned in 1980; its experience in nuclear work might or might not be a factor in the Navy's selection of another shipyard for nuclear certification—that is, if one was selected at all. See O'Rourke, Navy Nuclear-Powered Surface Ships.

[19] The Navy provided data to CBO in February 2009 on the cost of certification. CBO adjusted those data and allocated the $500 million certification cost equally among the ships in its hypothetical nuclear fleet.

[20] CBO used the average monthly price of imported oil delivered to U.S. refineries in its analysis.

[21] Prices in the first four months of this year have averaged $10 per barrel more than CBO forecast in January, and they could be higher or lower during the rest of the year. CBO expects to update its macroeconomic projections in August.

[22] The burden rate, reflecting the costs above the base cost of the fuel, is calculated in this instance as 178 divided by 86 minus 1.00.

[23] See Congressional Budget Office, Evaluating Military Compensation (June 2007). Veterans' benefits and some tax advantages for military personnel (certain allowances they receive are not subject to federal income tax) are not included in the defense budget but are instead reflected in higher outlays for other federal departments or in lower tax revenues. CBO has

nonetheless included those elements in its estimates because they reflect actual costs to U.S. taxpayers.

24. See Congressional Budget Office, The Long-Term Budget Outlook (June 2010, revised August 2010).

25. The Navy provided CBO with data on disposal costs in February 2009. Other estimates are available but would not substantially change CBO's findings; see, for example, Ronald O'Rourke, Navy Ship Acquisition: Options for Lower-Cost Ship Designs, Report for Congress RL32914 (Congressional Research Service, December 11, 2006), p. 16. In 2005, the Navy provided O'Rourke with an estimate of $70 million (in 2011 dollars) for deactivating, dismantling, and disposing of a retired nuclear-powered submarine; according to the Navy, work related to the reactor compartment would constitute roughly half of that total, or $35 million. The Navy also provided O'Rourke with a projection of about $1.1 billion (in 2011 dollars) for deactivating the nuclear-powered carrier U.S.S. Enterprise (CVN-65) in 2013. Work related to the ship's eight nuclear reactors accounted for about $730 million of the total.

26. CBO has applied the fair-value approach in other contexts; see, for example, Congressional Budget Office, Fannie Mae, Freddie Mac, and the Federal Role in the Secondary Mortgage Market (December 2010); The Budgetary Impact and Subsidy Costs of the Federal Reserve's Actions During the Financial Crisis (May 2010); and Costs and Policy Options for Federal Student Loan Programs (March 2010).

27. CBO's methodology for estimating discount rates is based on the capital asset pricing model, which is commonly used by private-sector analysts to select discount rates for long-run investment projects. For a discussion of the model, see Stephen Ross, Randolph Westerfield, and Jeffrey Jaffe, Corporate Finance (New York: McGraw-Hill/Irwin, 2009).

28. Kenneth J. Singleton, in a March 2011 unpublished manuscript ("Investor Flows and the 2008 Boom/Bust in Oil Prices"; www.stanford.edu/~kenneths/OilPub.pdf), discusses estimating risk premiums on the basis of information about expected future oil prices and the forward price curve for oil prices.

29. The return on Treasury bonds is consistent with CBO's long-term macroeconomic forecast of interest rates. The required return on oil investment, though numerically the same, was calculated by using a different methodology (described above), which adds a risk premium to an estimate of short-term interest rates.

End Notes for Appendix

1. For general information, see Office of Management and Budget, Guidelines and Discount Rates for Benefit-Cost Analysis of Federal Programs, Circular A-94 (October 29, 1992); for more specific information on past years' discount rates, see the table titled "Budget Assumptions: Nominal Treasury Interest Rates for Different Maturities (from the annual budget assumptions for the first year of the budget forecast)" in Appendix C of the circular (http://www.whitehouse.gov/sites/default/files/omb/assets dischist.pdf).

In: Navy Nuclear-Powered Surface Ships
Editors: R. Cabitta, M. Rocello

ISBN: 978-1-61470-790-5
© 2011 Nova Science Publishers, Inc.

Chapter 3

NAVY FORD (CVN-78) CLASS AIRCRAFT CARRIER PROGRAM: BACKGROUND AND ISSUES FOR CONGRESS[*]

Ronald O'Rourke

SUMMARY

CVN-78, CVN-79, and CVN-80 are the first three ships in the Navy's new Gerald R. Ford (CVN78) class of nuclear-powered aircraft carriers (CVNs).

CVN-78 was procured in FY2008 and is being funded with congressionally authorized four-year incremental funding in FY2008-FY2011. The Navy's proposed FY2012 budget estimates the ship's procurement cost at $11,531.0 million (i.e., about $11.5 billion) in then-year dollars. The Navy's proposed FY2011 budget requested $1,731.3 million in procurement funding as the final increment to complete this estimated procurement cost.

CVN-79 is scheduled for procurement in FY2013, and has received advance procurement funding since FY2007. The Navy's proposed FY2012 budget estimates the ship's procurement cost at $10,253.0 million (i.e., about $10.3 billion) in then-year dollars and requests $554.8 million in advance procurement funding for the ship.

---

[*] This is an edited, reformatted and augmented version of a Congressional Research Service publication, CRS Report for Congress RS20643, from www.crs.gov, dated April 12, 2011.

CVN-80 is scheduled for procurement in FY2018, with advance procurement funding scheduled to begin in FY2014. The Navy's proposed FY2012 budget estimates the ship's procurement cost at $13,494.9 million (i.e., about $13.5 billion) in then-year dollars.

On April 6, 2009, Secretary of Defense Robert Gates announced a number of recommendations he was making to the President for the FY2010 defense budget submission. One of these was to shift procurement of carriers to five-year intervals. This recommendation, which was included in the FY2010 defense budget submission, deferred the scheduled procurement of CVN-79 from FY2012 to FY2013, and the scheduled procurement of CVN-80 from FY2016 to FY2018. Secretary of Defense Robert Gates stated on April 6, 2009, that shifting carrier procurement to five-year intervals would put carrier procurement on "a more fiscally sustainable path."

Oversight issues for Congress for the CVN-78 program include technical risk and the potential for cost growth on CVNs 78, 79, and 80, and technical and design issues for CVN-78 class carriers that were raised in a December 2010 report from the Department of Defense (DOD) Director of Operational Test and Evaluation (DOT&E).

INTRODUCTION

CVN-78, CVN-79, and CVN-80 are the first three ships in the Navy's new Gerald R. Ford (CVN78) class of nuclear-powered aircraft carriers (CVNs). This report provides background information and potential oversight issues for Congress on the CVN-78 program.

BACKGROUND

The Navy's Aircraft Carrier Force

The Navy's aircraft carrier force consists of 11 nuclear-powered ships—the one-of-a-kind *Enterprise* (CVN-65), which entered service in 1961, and 10 Nimitz-class ships (CVNs 68 through 77) that entered service between 1975 and 2009. The most recently commissioned carrier, the *George H. W. Bush* (CVN-77), the final Nimitz-class ship, was procured in FY2001 and commissioned into service on January 10, 2009.[1] CVN-77 replaced the *Kitty Hawk* (CV-63), which was the Navy's last remaining conventionally powered carrier.[2]

Aircraft Carrier Construction Industrial Base

All U.S. aircraft carriers procured since FY1958 have been built by a Newport News, VA, shipyard that currently forms part of Northrop Grumman Shipbuilding (NGSB). Northrop's Newport News yard is the only U.S. shipyard that can build large-deck, nuclear-powered aircraft carriers. Northrop plans to spin off the Newport News yard and one of its other shipyards into a new independent firm some time in 2011. The aircraft carrier construction industrial base also includes hundreds of subcontractors and suppliers in dozens of states.

Gerald R. Ford (CVN-78) Class Program

The Gerald R. Ford (CVN-78) class carrier design is the successor to the Nimitz-class carrier design.[3] Compared to the Nimitz-class design, the Ford-class design will incorporate several improvements, including an ability to generate substantially more aircraft sorties per day and features permitting the ship to be operated by several hundred fewer sailors than a Nimitz-class ship, significantly reducing life-cycle operating and support costs. Navy plans call for procuring at least three Ford-class carriers—CVN-78, CVN-79, and CVN-80.

CVN-78

CVN-78, which was named in 2007 for President Gerald R. Ford,[4] was procured in FY2008 and is being funded with congressionally authorized four-year incremental funding in FY2008- FY2011.[5] The Navy's proposed FY2012 budget estimates the ship's procurement cost at $11,531.0 million (i.e., about $11.5 billion) in then-year dollars. The Navy's proposed FY2011 budget requested $1,731.3 million in procurement funding as the final increment to complete this estimated procurement cost.

CVN-78 is scheduled to enter service as the replacement for *Enterprise* (CVN-65). The Navy projects that there will be a 33-month period between the scheduled decommissioning of *Enterprise* in November 2012 and the scheduled commissioning of CVN-78 in September 2015. During this 33-month period, the Navy's carrier force is to temporarily decline from 11 ships to 10 ships. Since 10 USC 5062(b) requires the Navy to maintain a force of at least 11 operational carriers, the Navy asked Congress for a temporary waiver of 10 USC 5062(b) to accommodate the 33-month period between the scheduled decommissioning of *Enterprise* and the scheduled commissioning of CVN-78. Section 1023 of the FY2010 defense authorization act (H.R. 2647/P.L. 111-84 of October 28, 2009) authorizes the waiver and requires the Secretary of Defense to submit a report on the operational risk of temporarily reducing the size of the carrier force.

CVN-79

CVN-79 is scheduled for procurement in FY2013, and has received advance procurement (AP) funding since FY2007. The Navy's proposed FY2012 budget estimates the ship's procurement cost at $10,253.0 million (i.e., about $10.3 billion) in then-year dollars and requests $554.8 million in AP funding for the ship.

On April 6, 2009, Secretary of Defense Robert Gates announced a number of recommendations he was making to the President for the FY2010 defense budget submission. One of these was to shift procurement of carriers to five-year intervals. This recommendation, which was included in the FY2010 defense budget submission, deferred the scheduled procurement of CVN-79 from FY2012 to FY2013. Gates stated in his April 9, 2009, address that shifting carrier procurement to five-year intervals would put carrier procurement on "a more fiscally sustainable path."[6] For further discussion, see **Appendix B** and **Appendix C**.

CVN-80

CVN-80 is scheduled for procurement in FY2018, with advance procurement funding scheduled to begin in FY2014. The Navy's proposed FY2012 budget estimates the ship's procurement cost at $13,494.9 million (i.e., about $13.5 billion) in then-year dollars. Secretary of Defense Gates' April 2009 recommendation to shift carrier procurement to five-year intervals (see above discussion of CVN-79) deferred the procurement of CVN-80 from FY2016 to FY2018.

Procurement Funding

Table 1 shows procurement funding for CVNs 78, 79, and 80. Each ship is being procured with several years of advance procurement (AP) funding, followed by four-year incremental procurement funding of the remainder of the ship's cost.[7] The funding profile for CVN-78, for example, includes AP funding in FY2001-FY2007, followed by four years of incremental procurement funding in FY2008-FY2011.

**Table 1. Procurement Funding for CVNs 78, 79, and 80
(Millions of then-year dollars, rounded to nearest tenth)**

FY	CVN-78	CVN-79	CVN-80	Total
FY01	21.7 (AP)	0	0	21.7
FY02	135.3 (AP)	0	0	135.3
FY03	395.5 (AP)	0	0	395.5
FY04	1,162.9 (AP)	0	0	1,162.9
FY05	623.1 (AP)	0	0	623.1
FY06	618.9 (AP)	0	0	618.9
FY07	735.8 (AP)	52.8 (AP)	0	788.6
FY08	2,685.0	123.5 (AP)	0	2,808.6
FY09	2,684.6	1,210.6 (AP)	0	3,895.1
FY10	737.0	482.9 (AP)	0	1,219.9
FY11 (requested)	1,731.3	908.3 (AP)	0	2,639.6
FY12 (requested)	0	554.8 (AP)	0	554.8
FY13 (projected)	0	1,942.4	0	1,942.4
FY14 (projected)	0	1,920.3	228.1 (AP)	2,148.4
FY15 (projected)	0	2,030.9	1,514.9 (AP)	3,545.8
FY16 (projected)	0	1,026.5	1,476.5 (AP)	2,503.0

Source: FY2009-FY2012 Navy budget submissions.
Notes: Figures may not add due to rounding. "AP" is advance procurement funding.

Increase in Estimated Unit Procurement Costs

As shown in Table 2, the estimated procurement costs of CVNs 78, 79, and 80 in the FY2011 budget submission are 10.3%, 11.5%, and 25.9% higher, respectively, in then-year dollars than those in the FY2009 budget submission.[8] Table 2 also shows that the estimated procurement costs of CVNs 79 and 80 in the FY2012 budget are 1.5% and 0.1% lower, respectively, than those in the FY2011 budget.

Table 2. Estimated Procurement Costs of CVNs 78, 79, and 80
(As shown in FY2009-FY2012 budgets, in millions of then-year dollars)

Budget	CVN-78		CVN-79		CVN-80	
	Estimated procurement cost	Scheduled fiscal year of procurement	Estimated procurement cost	Scheduled fiscal year of procurement	Estimated procurement cost	Scheduled fiscal year of procurement
FY09 budget	10,457.9	FY08	9,191.6	FY12	10,716.8	FY16
FY10 budget	10,845.8	FY08	n/a[a]	FY13[b]	n/a[a]	FY18[b]
FY11 budget	11,531.0	FY08	10,413.1	FY13	13,577.0	FY18
FY12 budget	11,531.0	FY08	10,253.0	FY13	13,494.9	FY18
% change:						
FY09 budget to FY10 budget	+3.7		n/a		n/a	
FY10 budget to FY11 budget	+6.3		n/a		n/a	
FY11 budget to FY12 budget	No change		1.5		- 0.1	
FY09 budget to FY12 budget	+10.3		+11.5		+25.9	

Source: FY2009, FY2010, and FY2011Navy budget submissions.

[a] n/a means not available; the FY2010 budget submission did not show estimated procurement costs for CVNs 79 and 80.

[b] The FY2010 budget submission did not show scheduled years of procurement for CVNs 79 and 80; the dates shown here for the FY2010 budget submission are inferred from the shift to five-year intervals for procuring carriers that was announced by Secretary of Defense Gates in his April 6, 2009, news conference regarding recommendations for the FY2010 defense budget.

The increases in the estimated procurement costs of CVNs 78, 79, and 80 since the FY2009 budget submission have at least four potential causes:

- one additional year of inflation being incorporated into the cost of CVN-79 as a result of its scheduled procurement being deferred from FY2012 to FY2013, and two years of additional inflation being incorporated into the cost of CVN-80 as a result of its scheduled procurement being deferred from FY2016 to FY2018;
- increases in projected annual rates of inflation;
- higher estimates of real (i.e., inflation-adjusted) material costs, real labor rates, or labor hours (given a certain position on the production learning curve) for building CVN-78 class carriers; and
- increased costs due to loss of learning and reduced spreading of fixed overhead costs resulting from shifting to five-year intervals for procuring carriers.

Procurement Cost Cap

Section 122 of the FY2007 defense authorization act (H.R. 5122/P.L. 109-364 of October 17, 2006) established a procurement cost cap for CVN-78 of $10.5 billion, plus adjustments for inflation and other factors, and a procurement cost cap for subsequent Ford-class carriers of $8.1 billion each, plus adjustments for inflation and other factors. The conference report (H.Rept. 109- 702 of September 29, 2006) on P.L. 109-364 discusses Section 122 on pages 551-552.

The Navy on February 19, 2010, notified the congressional defense committees that, after making permitted adjustments in the cost cap for inflation and other factors, the estimated cost of CVN78 was $224 million below the cost cap for that ship.[9] The Navy on April 19, 2010, informed CRS and the Congressional Budget Office (CBO) that, after making permitted adjustments in the cost cap for inflation and other factors, the estimated costs of CVN-79 and CVN-80 each were several hundred million dollars below the cost cap for those ships.[10]

ISSUES FOR CONGRESS

Oversight issues for Congress for the CVN-78 program include technical risk and the potential for cost growth on CVNs 78, 79, and 80, and technical and design issues for CVN-78 class carriers that were raised in a December

2010 report from the Department of Defense (DOD) Director of Operational Test and Evaluation (DOT&E).

Technical Risk and Potential for Additional Cost Growth

Another oversight issue for Congress for the CVN-78 program concerns potential for cost growth on CVNs 78, 79, and 80. One possible source of additional cost growth in CVN-78 is new technologies that are being developed for the ship, particularly the electromagnetic aircraft launch system (EMALS)—an electromagnetic (as opposed to the traditional steam-powered) aircraft catapult. Problems in developing EMALS or other technologies could delay the ship's completion and increase its development and/or procurement cost.

March 9, 2011, Hearing

At a March 9, 2011, hearing on Navy shipbuilding issues before the Seapower and Projection Forces subcommittee of the House Armed Services Committee, the following exchange occurred between Representative Akin, the chairman of the subcommittee, and Sean Stackley, the Assistant Secretary of the Navy for Research, Development, and Acquisition (i.e., the Navy's acquisition executive):

REPRESENTATIVE AKIN:
... one of the things we've been paying attention to is the EMALS systems on new carrier and that has to be built into the hull and everything, and I gather the timeline on that is pretty tight. How is that going and do you see any problems with that or not?
STACKLEY:
Yes, sir. We have—we have been managing EMALS to the smallest detail. We are very concerned about two years ago that the program was not on track. We placed basically—we have replaced the management team as well as ensure that the program is properly funded both to complete its development and also to support in-yard- need-dates for the CVN-78.
Today—today, we are at a point in system development that we have turned over to the shipyard which referred to as the green book which takes all the testing that's been conducted up at Lakehurst where we have a full-scale model in the ground that we've used to launch aircraft. So we've developed the test requirements, turned over that green book to

Newport News on schedule so that they can continue to build the CVN-78 to support the test program.

On the production side, we are carefully watching each of the components that need to be delivered to Newport News. We have two in particular. Two motor generator sets out of 12 that have very limited float on in-yard-need-date, but we don't see difficulties right now in terms of meeting that and all the other components have float on the order of four to six months.

So, tight, yes, closing manage [sic: closely managed], yes. I think the risk is acceptable absolutely. We have to yet to complete the STD testing that we, as I described, we launched aircraft off the Lakehurst system in December. They really do stress it and to drive learning early on and coming out of that. In fact, we have uncovered some dynamics associated between the system and the aircraft's performance that we've taken a pause to work on more on the software side of correcting that issue so that we can ...

AKIN:

Software in order to change the amount of force relative to distance that the system develops or ... ?

STACKLEY:

No, Sir. The – what's beautiful about the EMALS is it's very scalable in terms of you dial in the load that you're putting on it and what you want for speed when at the end of the runway and the EMALS will do the rest. What we discovered in moving away from a dead load to an F-18 is: EMALS is a long – it's a number of linear motors that are in series and then a hand off from linear motor to linear motor as the aircraft is accelerating. There's a slight gap. And that can be tuned in terms of the way you ramp up the load and where you drop it off to minimize that gap so it's not perceptible to the pilot.

So it's an example what were not able to pick up in dead load testing which put a pilot on aircraft and that's a report I received back until we docked in to that to figure out what the best way to mitigate that so that it's not a problem.

So the test program—bottom line is the test program is frankly in good shape. It is a fairly exhaustive test program. We did take a pause because we did not while we were working on these changes or corrections coming out of the live aircraft testing. We did not want to have a standing army on the test side that was performing inefficiently, so we took a pause; we're coming back with corrections and picking back up the system functional demonstration this month.[11]

March 2011 GAO Report

The Government Accountability office (GAO) reported the following in March 2011 regarding the status of the CVN-78 program, including the potential for cost growth:

Technology Maturity

Seven of the CVN 21 program's 13 current critical technologies have not been demonstrated in a realistic, at-sea environment. Of these technologies, EMALS, the advanced arresting gear, and dual band radar present the greatest risk to the ship's cost and schedule. Program officials stated that EMALS development has been one of the primary drivers of CVN 78 cost increases. Problems have occurred in EMALS testing which could result in more design changes later in the program. Testing uncovered a crack in the motor, which has already resulted in several design changes; and in January 2010, a motor controller software error caused damage to the EMALS hardware. Both fixes have successfully been retested. The program completed the first four F/A-18E launches in December 2010. The advanced arresting gear is nearing maturity and has completed extended reliability testing. However, delays in land-based testing with simulated and live aircraft could lead to late delivery. The Navy finalized a fixed-price production contract for EMALS and the advanced arresting gear in June 2010. Although the Navy continues to pay design and testing costs, any EMALS changes identified during development will be incorporated into the production units at no cost to the government. The dual band radar, which includes the volume search and multifunction radars, is being developed by the DDG 1000 destroyer program and is also nearing maturity. However, as a part of a program restructuring, the DDG 1000 eliminated the volume search radar from the program. According to Navy officials, radar development has not been affected, but CVN 78 will now be the first ship to operate with this radar. Radar equipment will be delivered for installation and testing beginning September 2011 for the multifunction radar and in January 2012 for the volume search radar.

Design Maturity

In September 2008, CVN 78 began production with only 76 percent of its three-dimensional product model complete. The three-dimensional product model was completed by November 2009, but the contractor is currently making design changes to prevent electrical cable routing from interfering with other design features. As EMALS and other systems complete testing, additional design changes may be necessary.

Production Maturity

The Navy awarded the CVN 78 construction contract in September 2008. Construction of approximately 65 percent of the ship's structural units is complete. These units account for about 19 percent of the ship's total production hours. As of July 2010, construction of the hull in dry dock was behind schedule because of late material deliveries from suppliers.

Other Program Issues

In 2010, the CVN 21 program shifted from a 4- to 5-year build cycle, which could increase program costs. According to program officials, the shipbuilder projects that this change will increase costs by 9 to 15 percent due to the loss of learning and effect on the supplier base, among other inefficiencies. The Navy disagrees with this assessment and reported to Congress that the shift will have minimal negative consequences. The dual band radar also presents cost risks for the program. Program officials are considering buying the radar for both CVN 79 and CVN 80 at the same time, in order to reduce the risks associated with the production line being idle for up to 5 years. However, this strategy could lead to increased costs if changes identified during at-sea testing on CVN 78 need to be incorporated into the already-procured systems for the two follow-on ships.

Program Office Comments

In commenting on a draft of this assessment, the Navy generally concurred with this assessment. Officials stated the program is addressing the technology and construction challenges for a successful September 2015 delivery, and that CVN 79 is on track to award a construction contract by the first quarter fiscal year 2013. The Navy stated that while the change from a 4- to 5-year build cycle will increase the unit cost of the CVN 78 class carrier, it facilitates a reduced average yearly funding requirement over a longer period of time. The Navy also provided technical comments, which were incorporated as appropriate.[12]

June 30, 2010, Selected Acquisition Report

DOD's June 30, 2010, Selected Acquisition Report (SAR) for the CVN-78 program states:

> Electromagnetic Aircraft Launch System component production remains on schedule to support CVN 78 construction with subsystems deliveries meeting Required In-Yard Dates. The first two, of three, phases of the High Cycle Testing are complete. The third phase is scheduled for completion in September 2010. The first of two phases of the Highly Accelerated Life Testing is complete. The second phase is planned for a September 2011 completion. System Functional Demonstration is scheduled to begin in September 2010, with live aircraft launching planned for Late Fall 2010.[13]

May 2010 CBO Report

A May 2010 CBO report on the potential cost of the Navy's FY2011 30-year shipbuilding plan states:

> The Navy's projected cost of the lead ship of the CVN-78 class grew by 10 percent between the President's 2008 and 2011 budget requests. The Navy now expects the lead ship's cost to be about $11.7 billion (about what CBO estimated in its analysis of the Navy's 2009 plan). Yet further increases appear likely. The CVN-78 is only about 10 percent complete, and cost growth in shipbuilding programs typically occurs when a ship is more than half finished— particularly in the later stages of construction, when all of a ship's systems must be installed and integrated.
>
> To estimate the cost of the lead ship of the CVN-78 class, CBO used the actual costs of the previous carrier—the CVN-77—and then adjusted them for higher costs for government-furnished equipment and for more than $3 billion in costs for nonrecurring engineering and detail design (the plans, drawings, and other one-time items associated with the first ship of a new class). As a result, CBO estimates that the lead CVN-78 will cost about $12.5 billion once it is completed. Subsequent ships of the class will not require as much funding for onetime items; however, on the basis of higher projected inflation in shipbuilding costs, CBO estimates the average cost of the six carriers in the 2011 plan at $12.4 billion, whereas the Navy estimates their average cost at $10.6 billion....
>
> There are several reasons to believe that the final cost of the CVN-78 could be even higher than CBO's estimate. First, most lead ships built in the past 20 years have experienced cost growth of more than 40 percent. (CBO's estimate for the lead CVN-78 already accounts for some of that historical cost growth.) Second, Navy officials have told CBO that there is a 60 percent probability that the final cost of the CVN-78 will exceed the service's estimate, compared with a 40 percent probability that the final cost will be less than that estimate. Third, a number of critical technologies that are supposed to be incorporated into the ship, such as a new electromagnetic catapult system for launching aircraft, remain under development. Difficulties in completing their development could arise and increase costs, which would affect the costs for subsequent ships of the class.[14]

Technical and Design Issues—December 2010 DOT&E Report

A December 2010 report on various DOD acquisition programs from DOD's Director, Operational Test and Evaluation (DOT&E)—DOT&E's annual report for FY2010—stated, in its section on the CVN-78 program, that

> The CVN 78 program continues to have challenges with F-35 Joint Strike Fighter (JSF) integration. The thermal footprint from the main engine exhaust, shipboard noise levels, and information technology requirements need work. Design changes may be required for the jet blast deflectors, and active cooling may be required in the flight deck just forward of the jet blast deflector....
> Numerous integrated warfare system items are of concern, including:
> - The ship-self-defense combat systems on aircraft carriers have historically had reliability and weapon system integration shortcomings. While the Navy has made efforts, it has not yet developed a detailed plan to address these concerns on CVN 78.
> - The Navy lags in developing a new anti-ship ballistic missile target and in obtaining a capability to launch four simultaneous supersonic sea-skimming targets. Both are required to assess effectiveness of ship self-defense....
>
> EMALS experienced two notable hardware/software incidents that caused test delays at the SFD [System Functional Design] test site at Lakehurst [NJ]. One incident involved an uncommanded armature retraction due to a software anomaly in the asset protection module. The second anomaly involved the loss of an encoder from the catapult armature during a dead-load test. Both anomalies have been resolved. EMALS has started performance verification with dead loads at the SFD site, and [the] AAG [Advanced Arresting Gear] is nearing the start of Jet Car Track Site dead load testing. Required In Yard Date (RIYD) for these systems continues to drive the development schedule; however, to date development and testing remains on track.[15]

LEGISLATIVE ACTIVITY FOR FY2012

As shown in Table 1, the Navy's proposed FY2012 budget requests $554.8 million in advance procurement funding for CVN-79.

APPENDIX A. LEGISLATIVE ACTIVITY FOR FY2011

FY2011 Funding Request

The Navy proposed FY2011 budget requested $1,731.3 million in procurement funding for CVN78 and $908.3 million in advance procurement funding for CVN-79.

FY2011 DOD and Full-Year Continuing Appropriations Act (H.R. 1473)

According to line-item funding tables posted by the House Rules Committee,[16] the FY2011 Department of Defense and Full-Year Continuing Appropriations Act (H.R. 1473 of the 112th Congress, introduced on April 11, 2011) reduces the Navy's request for FY2011 procurement funding for CVN-78 by $9.287 million, and fully funds the Navy's request for FY2011 advance procurement funding for CVN-79. The reduction of $9.287 million in procurement funding for CVN-78 includes $2.6 million for "Consolidated Afloat Navy Enterprise System Increment 1," $4.9 million for "Surface Electronic Warfare Improvement," and $1.787 million for "AN/UPX29."

FY2011 DOD Appropriations Act (S. 3800)

The Senate Appropriations Committee, in its report (S.Rept. 111-295 of September 16, 2010) on S. 3800 of the 111th Congress, recommended approval of the Navy's request for FY2011 procurement and advance procurement funding for CVN-78 and CVN-79 (page 86).

FY2011 Defense Authorization Act (H.R. 6523/P.L. 111-383)

House (H.R. 5136)

The House Armed Services Committee, in its report (H.Rept. 111-491 of May 21, 2010) on the FY2011 defense authorization bill (H.R. 5136), recommended approval of the Navy's request for FY2011 procurement and advance procurement funding for CVN-78 and CVN-79 (page 73).

Section 1021 of H.R. 5136 as reported by the committee would amend the law (10 USC 231) that requires the Department of Defense to annually submit a 30-year Navy shipbuilding plan. The amendment would, among other things, require that the Secretary of the Navy, in submitting each 30-year plan, "ensure that such plan—(1) is in accordance with section 5062(b) of this title [i.e., 10 USC 5062(b), which requires the Navy to maintain a force of at least 11 operational carriers]; and (2) phases the construction of new aircraft carriers during the periods covered by such plan in a manner that minimizes the total cost for procurement for such vessels."

The committee's report states:

Aircraft carriers

The committee is concerned that the decision by the Secretary of Defense in April 2009, prior to the completion of the congressionally mandated analysis of the Quadrennial Defense Review, to shift aircraft carrier construction to five-year centers for the stated purpose of "a more fiscally sustainable path" was shortsighted. The committee has recently learned via receipt of Department of Defense Selected Acquisition Reports that the cost to construct the next three Ford-class aircraft carriers is likely to increase by up to $4.0 billion because of the change in construction centers. The committee notes that the current 30-year shipbuilding plan would not maintain a force of 11 operational aircraft carriers past fiscal year 2040 and therefore does not conform to the requirement in section 5062b of title 10, United States Code, to maintain an operational fleet of 11 aircraft carriers.

The committee expects that subsequent plans will conform to current law, or the Secretary of the Navy will request a change to statute commensurate with detailed analysis of the effect a reduction to 10 operational aircraft carriers will have on the national military strategy. In title I [sic: Title X – Section 1021] of this Act, the committee directs the Secretary of Defense to phase the construction of aircraft carriers to minimize the total cost for procurement of the vessels. (Page 75)

Senate (S. 3454)

The FY2011 defense authorization bill (S. 3454), as reported by the Senate Armed Services Committee (S.Rept. 111-201 of June 4, 2010), recommended approval of the Navy's request for FY2011 procurement and advance procurement funding for CVN-78 and CVN-79 (see page 677 of the printed bill).

Final Version (H.R. 6523/P.L. 111-383)
Section 102(a)(3) of H.R. 6523/P.L. 111-383 of January 7, 2011, authorized FY2011 funding for the Navy's entire shipbuilding account at the requested amount. H.R. 6523 contains no provisions relating specifically to procurement of aircraft carriers. The joint explanatory statement of the House and Senate Armed Services Committees on H.R. 6523 does not discuss procurement of aircraft carriers.

APPENDIX B. EARLIER OVERSIGHT ISSUE: SHIFT TO FIVE-YEAR INTERVALS: A MORE FISCALLY SUSTAINABLE PATH?

On April 6, 2009, Secretary of Defense Robert Gates announced a number of recommendations he was making to the President for the FY2010 defense budget submission. One of these was to shift procurement of carriers to five-year intervals. This recommendation, which was included in the FY2010 defense budget submission, deferred the scheduled procurement of CVN-79 from FY2012 to FY2013, and the scheduled procurement of CVN-80 from FY2016 to FY2018.

Gates stated in his April 9, 2009, address that shifting carrier procurement to five-year intervals would put carrier procurement on "a more fiscally sustainable path."[17] This was interpreted as meaning that shifting to five-year intervals (compared to a combination of four- and five-year intervals in previous Navy 30-year shipbuilding plans) would reduce the average amount of funding required each year for procuring carriers.

As a simplified notional example, if carriers are assumed to cost $10 billion each, then shifting from a four-year interval to a five-year interval would reduce the average amount of carrier procurement funding needed each year from $2.5 billion to $2.0 billion, a reduction of $500 million per year.

This simplified notional example, however, assumes that shifting from four- to five-year intervals does not by itself cause an increase in the real (i.e., inflation-adjusted) procurement cost of the carriers. Increasing the procurement interval could by itself cause an increase in the real procurement cost of the carriers by reducing learning-curve benefits (i.e., causing a loss of learning) from one carrier to the next, and by reducing the spreading of fixed overhead costs at the Newport News shipyard and at supplier firms. A real increase in carrier procurement costs due to such effects would offset at least some of the reduction in the average amount of carrier procurement funding needed each year that would result from shifting to five-year intervals.

Shifting to five-year intervals for procuring carriers could also increase the costs of other Navy ship programs. NGSB's Newport News shipyard performs mid-life nuclear refueling complex overhauls (RCOHs) on Nimitz-class carriers, and jointly builds Virginia-class nuclear-powered attack submarines along with another shipyard (General Dynamics' Electric Boat Division). In addition, vendors that make nuclear-propulsion components for carriers make analogous components for nuclear-powered submarines. A reduced spreading of fixed costs at NGSB's Newport News yard and at nuclear-propulsion component vendors due to the shift to five-year intervals for carrier procurement might thus also increase costs for Nimitz-class RCOHs and Virginia-class submarines. Increases in costs for these programs would further offset the reduction in the average amount of carrier procurement funding needed each year that would result from shifting to five-year intervals for carrier procurement.

Potential key oversight questions for Congress included the following:

- How much of the increase since the FY2009 budget submission in the estimated procurement costs of CVNs 78, 79, and 80 (see Table 2) is due to the shift to five-year intervals for procuring carriers?
- How do potential increases in the costs of CVN-78 class aircraft carriers, Nimitzclass RCOHs, and Virginia-class submarines caused by the shift to five-year intervals for procuring carriers affect the calculation of the net change in average annual funding requirements that results from shifting carrier procurement to five-year intervals?

May 2009 Northrop Grumman Shipbuilding Statement

A May 2009 Northrop Grumman Shipbuilding statement on the cost impact of shifting to five-year intervals for procuring carriers states:

> One element of the announcement by the Secretary of Defense last week was to shift from four (4) years to five (5) years between construction start for each new Ford Class carrier. Past Northrop Grumman Shipbuilding experience with carrier new construction has shown that the optimum time between carrier construction is less than 4 years. This allows the most efficient flow of the work force from one ship to the next, and facilitates a learning curve for carriers. Moving to five (5)

year intervals between starts will require the shipyard to sub-optimize manning level sequencing and result in added trade training, loss of learning, and added startup costs.

Increasing the time between carrier construction can have a large impact on the supplier base, driving cost increases of 5-10 percent, or higher in some cases, above normal escalation. Material costs of suppliers who provide similar components to other Navy programs currently under contract will also experience cost growth. Some equipment suppliers can be expected to exit the market as a result of the additional year with the expense of component requalification being realized.

Finally, the decrease in production labor volume on an annual basis, created by the increase in the time interval between carrier construction starts will increase the cost to other programs in the yard. This applies to work already under contract, namely Virginia class submarines (VCS) Block 2 and Block 3, and CVN 78 predominately; and for future work not yet under contract, namely Carrier RCOH's, CVN79 and follow-on Ford class carrier construction, and later Blocks of VCS. The impact to work already under contract is expected to be in the range of $100M of cost growth. We also expect cost increases for future contracts yet to be priced. Conservative projections of the shipbuilder cost impact to CVN 79 and CVN80 for the one year delay will be on the order of a 9-15 percent cost increase.[18]

March 2010 GAO Report

A March 2010 GAO report stated that if carrier procurement were shifted to five-year intervals, "the fabrication start date for CVN 80 will be delayed by 2 years, which will increase the amount of shipyard overhead costs paid under the CVN 79 contract."[19]

March 2010 Navy Report Required by Section 126

Section 126 of the FY2010 defense authorization act (H.R. 2647/P.L. 111-84 of October 28, 2009) required the Secretary of the Navy to submit a report to the congressional defense committees on the effects of using a five-year interval for the construction of Ford-class aircraft carriers. The conference report (H.Rept. 111-288 of October 7, 2009) on H.R. 2647/P.L. 111-84 stated the following regarding Section 126:

The conferees note that a 5-year interval for aircraft carrier construction, as proposed by the Secretary of Defense, may be the appropriate course of action for the Department of the Navy. However, the conferees are concerned that this decision may not have been made following a rigorous cost-benefit analysis. Therefore, the conferees expect that the Secretary of the Navy will take no further action to preclude the ability of the Secretary to award a construction contract for CVN–79 in fiscal year 2012 or the aircraft carrier designated CVN– 80 in fiscal year 2016, consistent with the Annual Long-Range Plan for Construction of Naval Vessels for Fiscal Year 2009, until he completes the required assessment and fully informs the congressional defense committees of any such a decision. (Page 680)

The Navy submitted the report on March 4, 2010.[20] The report states, among other things, that

- "It is reasonable to assume that some vendor base inefficiencies, in addition to inflation may occur by increasing CVN build intervals to five years."
- "While a five-year interval between carrier construction starts will result in potential inefficiencies and gaps for specific carrier construction trade skills, the Navy plans to closely manage the transition to 5-year centers to minimize the impact of this change on training of individuals required to support ship construction."
- "The Navy estimated that a four-year build interval would maximize the opportunity to achieve labor efficiencies due to learning. A five-year build interval reduces this opportunity; however, the overall impact for loss of learning associated with a shift to five-year centers is manageable through Advance Procurement and Advance Construction."
- "The Navy assessed the NIMITZ Class cost returns for shipbuilder labor and material and GFE to determine the correlation between these cost elements and the number of years between carrier awards. The Navy estimates that impact to Basic Construction is around 1.0% for CVN 79 and CVN 80."
- "The change to five-year build intervals results in an overhead decrease in direct labor workload for aircraft carrier construction, thereby causing the overhead rates to increase proportionately. The Navy estimates the construction portion increase is less than 1% each for CVN 78, CVN 79 and CVN 80."

- "The impact of changing the interval between carrier awards to the VIRGINIA Class submarine current Block II and Block III contracts is estimated to be $30- 50 million per hull."[21]

The report does not provide an overall dollar calculation of how much of the increase since the FY2009 budget submission in the estimated procurement costs of CVNs 78, 79, and 80 is due to the shift to five-year intervals for procuring carriers. Virginia-class submarines are scheduled to be procured at a rate of two ships per year starting FY2011. If the cost increase of $30 million to $50 million for each Virginia-class boat cited in the Navy's report holds for Virginia-class boats procured in FY2011 and subsequent years, then the shift to five-year intervals for procuring carriers would increase Virginia-class procurement costs by $60 million to $100 million per year.

For the text of the Navy's report, see **Appendix C**.

June 30, 2010, Selected Acquisition Report (SAR)

The Department of Defense's (DOD's) June 30, 2010, Selected Acquisition Report (SAR) for the CVN-78 program states that the estimated increase in Ford-class procurement costs resulting from shifting to five-year intervals for procuring carriers is $1,798.0 million in then-year dollars, consisting of $521.0 million for CVN-79 and $1,277.0 million for CVN-80.[22] The June 30, 2010, SAR states that these two figures are a "clarification" of figures presented in the December 31, 2009, SAR. The December 31, 2009, SAR estimated the increase at $4,131.2 million in then-year dollars, consisting of $1,131.4 million for CVN-79 and $2,999.8 million CVN-80, but also stated that these figures were "overstated, and will be corrected in the June 2010 SAR."[23] The difference between the June 30, 2010, SAR, and the December 31, 2009, SAR regarding the estimated increase in procurement costs resulting from shifting to five-year intervals for procuring carriers (i.e., $4,131.2 million minus $1,798.0 million) is $2,333.2 million. The June 30, 2010, SAR re-attributes a net total of $2,333.2 million in estimated cost increases to factors other than shifting to five-year intervals for procuring carriers, and reports total estimated procurement costs for CVN-79 and CVN-80 that are the same as those reported in the December 31, 2009, SAR. Neither the June 30, 2010, SAR nor the December 31, 2009, SAR shows an estimated increase in the procurement cost for CVN-78 resulting from shifting to five-year intervals for procuring carriers. The figures in the June 30, 2010, SAR are consistent with the Navy-provided figures presented in Table B-1.

Navy Data Provided to CRS and CBO on June 24, 2010

On April 19, 2010, following a Navy briefing to CRS and CBO on the CVN-78 program, CRS asked the Navy to provide the procurement costs of CVNs 78, 79, and 80 in constant FY2011 dollars as in the proposed FY2011 budget, and what these costs would have been in the proposed FY2011 budget if there had been no shift to five-year intervals for carrier procurement (i.e., if CVN-79 were procured in FY2012 and CVN-80 were procured in FY2016). The Navy provided the figures (in both then-year and constant FY2011 dollars) to CRS and CBO on June 24, 2010. Table B-1 shows the figures.

Table B-1. Cost Impact of Shifting to Five-year Intervals
(Millions of dollars, rounded to nearest tenth)

	CVN-78	CVN-79	CVN-80
Then-year dollars			
Cost in FY2011 budget	11,531.0	10,413.1	13,577.0
What the figure would have been in FY2011 budget if there had been no shift to five-year intervals	11,531.0	9,892.1	12,300.0
Difference (dollars)	0	521.0	1,277.0
Difference (%)	0	5.3%	10.4%
Constant FY2011 dollars			
Cost in FY2011 budget	11,875.9	9,742.3	11,628.5
What the figure would have been in FY2011 budget if there had been no shift to five-year intervals	11,875.9	9,396.7	10,872.2
Difference (dollars)	0	345.6	756.3
Difference (%)	0	3.7%	7.0%

Source: Briefing slide entitled "CVN 78 Class CBO/CRS Data Request," dated June 24, 2010, and provided as an attachment to a Navy information paper dated May 19, 2010. The May 19, 2010, information paper and the June 24, 2010, attachment were provided to CRS and CBO on June 24, 2010.

Notes: In the scenario assuming there had been no shift to five-year intervals for carrier procurement, CVN-79 would be procured in FY2012 and CVN-80 would be procured in FY2016. The Navy converted then-year dollars to constant FY2011 dollars using a January 2010 SCN (i.e., shipbuilding budget) deflator. FY2011 budget figures for CVN-80 reflect a CVN-78 program estimate pending official approval from the Naval Sea Systems Command (NAVSEA).

APPENDIX C. TEXT OF NAVY REPORT ON EFFECTS OF SHIFTING TO FIVE-YEAR INTERVALS

The following is the text of the Navy's report on the effects of shifting to five-year intervals for procuring carriers.[24]

I. REPORT REQUIREMENTS

Section 126 of the National Defense Authorization Act for Fiscal Year 2010, P.L. 111-84, (hereinafter "Section 126") requires that a report be submitted to Congress no later than February 1, 2010 assessing the effects of using a five-year interval for the construction of Gerald R. Ford Class aircraft carriers. The assessment shall include impacts with respect to four specified areas resulting from this change in acquisition strategy. This report fulfills the Navy's reporting obligation pursuant to Section 126. The language of this section is as follows:

"Not later than February 1, 2010, the Secretary of the Navy shall submit to the congressional defense committees a report on the effects of using a five-year interval for the construction of FORD Class aircraft carriers. The report shall include, at a minimum, an assessment of the effects of such five-year interval on the following:

(1) With respect to the supplier base-

(A) the viability of the base, including suppliers exiting the market or other potential reductions in competition; and

cost increases to the Ford Class aircraft carrier program.

(2) Training of individuals in trades related to ship construction.

(3) Loss of expertise associated with ship construction.

(4) The costs of—

(A) any additional technical support or production planning associated with the start of construction;

(B) material and labor;

(C) overhead; and

(D) other ship construction programs, including the costs of existing and future contracts."

II. ASSESSMENT DISCUSSION

On April 6, 2009, Secretary of Defense announced within a Defense Budget Recommendation Statement that the Navy's CVN 21 aircraft carrier program (Ford Class) would shift from a four-year to a five-year build cycle, thereby placing the program on a more fiscally sustainable path. This will result in 10 aircraft carriers after 2040. The five-year build cycle allows for a balance between carrier build-rate and inventory, and a more effective use of overall Shipbuilding and Conversion, Navy funding between carrier programs and other ship, submarine, support, and amphibious ship recapitalization plans.

1. IMPACT TO SUPPLIER BASE

It has been the Navy's experience that longstanding aircraft carrier suppliers have generally responded to ship construction schedule shifts and extended workload gaps without widespread disruption or loss of continuity for critical products from most vendors. For example, the interval between procurement of CVN 77 and CVN 78 was originally planned to be five years, but grew to seven years. There was no significant impact on the shipbuilder's procurement of components to support ship construction.

In addition, for a 2009 Navy-funded RAND Corporation study, RAND sought comments from 46 major suppliers regarding the impact of moving the CVN 79 award date to Fiscal Year 2013. The suppliers chosen were those deemed critical to aircraft carrier construction by the shipbuilder. The majority of the 18 major suppliers who responded indicated that less than 20% of their total annual revenues were from aircraft carrier construction, and nearly all responding vendors indicated they provide services to other Navy ship platforms including submarines, surface combatants, and aircraft carrier Refueling and Complex Overhauls (RCOH). It is reasonable to assume that some vendor base inefficiencies, in addition to inflation may occur by increasing CVN build intervals to five years. Efforts by the Navy to drive cross-platform commonality of parts and proactively manage obsolescence also mitigate the risk of economic dependence. As a result, economic dependence on Ford Class aircraft carrier order frequency for the majority of the vendor industrial base is projected to be low. The Navy plans to continue to closely manage this industrial base to minimize impacts and costs.

2-3. IMPACT TO TRAINING AND EXPERTISE

The construction start of the Ford Class coincides with an overall ramp-up in shipyard production efforts in the Fiscal Year 2010-Fiscal Year 2013 timeframe due to an increase to two per year VIRGINIA Class submarines, more consistent carrier build frequencies, sustained NIMITZ Class RCOH program, and the start of CVN 65 inactivation. While a five-year interval between carrier construction starts will result in potential inefficiencies and gaps for specific carrier construction trade skills, the Navy plans to closely manage the transition to 5- year centers to minimize the impact of this change on training of individuals required to support ship construction.

The Navy estimated that a four-year build interval would maximize the opportunity to achieve labor efficiencies due to learning. A five-year build interval reduces this opportunity; however, the overall impact for loss of learning associated with a shift to five-year centers is manageable through Advance Procurement and Advance Construction.

4. COST IMPACTS

There are three primary sources of cost impact associated with increasing the intervals between carrier construction starts - inflation, inefficiencies, and overhead impacts. The effects of these are addressed in paragraphs 4A, 4B, and 4C for CVN 79 and CVN 80. For other work at the shipyard, the collective impacts of the three sources are provided in paragraph 4D.

A. Cost of any Additional Technical Support or Production Planning Associated with the Start of Construction

Since CVN 79 advance planning and procurement commenced prior to the five-year build interval decision, CVN 79 technical support and production planning will be adjusted for the five-year interval. The Construction Preparation contract will be extended by one year to meet the construction award shift from Fiscal Year 2012 to Fiscal Year 2013. With the exception of costs associated with an additional year of planning amounting to about 1%, there should be no other fiscal implications with this extension.

B. Cost of Material and Labor

A five-year build interval imposes one additional year of inflation on the CVN 79 and two additional years on CVN 80. The Navy estimates a 3% impact on the Basic Construction Cost and Government Furnished Equipment (GFE) for CVN 79 and an 8% impact to CVN 80. This inflation impact will be addressed in the budget request for these two ships.

The Navy assessed the NIMITZ Class cost returns for shipbuilder labor and material and GFE to determine the correlation between these cost elements and the number of years between carrier awards. The Navy estimates that impact to Basic Construction is around 1.0% for CVN 79 and CVN 80.

C. Cost of Overhead

Overhead rates (percentage of direct labor) at the shipbuilder and major suppliers are directly correlated to the projected direct labor workload. The change to five-year build intervals results in an overall decrease in direct labor workload for aircraft carrier construction, thereby causing the overhead rates to increase proportionally. The Navy estimates the construction portion increase is less than 1% each for CVN 78, CVN 79 and CVN 80. The Navy will be working with the shipbuilder on managing overhead in the shipyard.

D. Costs of Other Ship Construction Programs, Including the Costs of Existing and Future Contracts

The impact of changing the interval between carrier awards to the VIRGINIA Class submarine current Block II and Block III contracts is estimated to be $30-50 million per hull. The increase in costs is associated with workload reallocatjon in the shipbuilding industrial base.

III. REPORT SUMMARY

This report, as required by Section 126 of P.L. 111-84, assesses the impacts resulting from the shift of the acquisition schedule to five-year intervals for Ford Class aircraft carriers. A review of available information indicates there will be a minimal impact on the supplier base if closely managed. Since the shipyard has ample opportunity to plan for five-year intervals, any impacts to worker training or trade skill inefficiencies, and workload planning is assessed to be manageable.

The change from a four-year to a five-year build interval will result in a unit cost increase to the Ford Class carriers that have funding requirements in the Future Years Defense Program. The Navy is continuing to refine the estimated impacts and will adjust future budget submissions. These increases are due primarily to inflation, inefficiencies, and overhead adjustments that will be factored into the overall budget request for each ship. Despite the inflation adjusted costs per ship, the change in build interval allows carrier annual funding requirements to be spread over longer periods of time, maintains a steady state 11 carrier force structure until after 2040, and facilitates a reduced average annual aircraft carrier funding requirement.

End Notes

[1] Congress approved $4,053.7 million in FY2001 procurement funding to complete CVN-77's then-estimated total procurement cost of $4,974.9 million. Section 122 of the FY1998 defense authorization act (H.R. 1119/P.L. 105-85 of November 18, 1997) limited the ship's procurement cost to $4.6 billion, plus adjustments for inflation and other factors. The Navy testified in 2006 that with these permitted adjustments, the cost cap stood at $5.357 billion. The Navy also testified that CVN-77's estimated construction cost had increased to $6.057 billion, or $700 million above the adjusted cost cap. Consequently, the Navy in 2006 requested that Congress increase the cost cap to $6.057 billion. Congress approved this request: Section 123 of the FY2007 defense authorization act (H.R. 5122/P.L. 109-364 of October 17, 2006), increased the cost cap for CVN-77 to $6.057 billion.

[2] The *Kitty Hawk* was decommissioned on January 31, 2009.

[3] The CVN-78 class was earlier known as the CVN-21 class, which meant nuclear-powered aircraft carrier for the 21st century.

[4] Section 1012 of the FY2007 defense authorization act (H.R. 5122/P.L. 109-364 of October 17, 2006) expressed the sense of the Congress that CVN-78 should be named for President

Gerald R. Ford. On January 16, 2007, the Navy announced that CVN-78 would be so named. CVN-78 and other carriers built to the same design will consequently be referred to as Ford (CVN-78) class carriers. For further discussion of Navy ship names, see CRS Report RS22478, *Navy Ship Names: Background for Congress*, by Ronald O'Rourke.

[5] Section 121 of the FY2007 defense authorization act (H.R. 5122/P.L. 109-364 of October 17, 2006) granted the Navy the authority to use four-year incremental funding for CVN-78, CVN-79, and CVN-80.

[6] Source: Statement of Secretary of Defense Robert Gates, at April 6, 2009, news conference on his recommendations for the FY2010 defense budget.

[7] As noted earlier, Section 121 of the FY2007 defense authorization act (H.R. 5122/P.L. 109-364 of October 17, 2006) granted the Navy the authority to use four-year incremental funding for CVN-78, CVN-79, and CVN-80.

[8] CBO in 2008 and the Government Accountability Office (GAO) in 2007 questioned the accuracy of the Navy's cost estimate for CVN-78. CBO reported in June 2008 that it estimated that CVN-78 would cost $11.2 billion in constant FY2009 dollars, or about $900 million more than the Navy's estimate of $10.3 billion in constant FY2009 dollars, and that if "CVN-78 experienced cost growth similar to that of other lead ships that the Navy has purchased in the past 10 years, costs could be much higher still." CBO also reported that, although the Navy publicly expressed confidence in its cost estimate for CVN-78, the Navy had assigned a confidence level of less than 50% to its estimate, meaning that the Navy believed there was more than a 50% chance that the estimate would be exceeded. (Congressional Budget Office, *Resource Implications of the Navy's Fiscal Year 2009 Shipbuilding Plan*, June 9, 2008, p. 20.) GAO reported in August 2007 that: Costs for CVN 78 will likely exceed the budget for several reasons. First, the Navy's cost estimate, which underpins the budget, is optimistic. For example, the Navy assumes that CVN 78 will be built with fewer labor hours than were needed for the previous two carriers. Second, the Navy's target cost for ship construction may not be achievable. The shipbuilder's initial cost estimate for construction was 22 percent higher than the Navy's cost target, which was based on the budget. Although the Navy and the shipbuilder are working on ways to reduce costs, the actual costs to build the ship will likely increase above the Navy's target. Third, the Navy's ability to manage issues that affect cost suffers from insufficient cost surveillance. Without effective cost surveillance, the Navy will not be able to identify early signs of cost growth and take necessary corrective action. (Government Accountability Office, Defense Acquisitions[:] Navy Faces Challenges Constructing the Aircraft Carrier Gerald R. Ford within Budget, GAO-07-866, August 2007, summary page. See also Government Accountability Office, Defense Acquisitions[:] Realistic Business Cases Needed to Execute Navy Shipbuilding Programs, Statement of Paul L. Francis, Director, Acquisition and Sourcing Management Team, Testimony Before the Subcommittee on Seapower and Expeditionary Forces, Committee on Armed Services, House of Representatives, July 24, 2007 (GAO-07-943T), p. 15.)

[9] Source: Letter dated February 19, 2010, from Secretary of the Navy Ray Mabus to the chairmen of the House and Senate Armed Services committees and the Defense subcommittees of the House and Senate Appropriations Committees. Copy of letter provided by the Navy to CRS and the Congressional Budget Office (CBO) on April 19, 2010.

[10] Source: April 19, 2010, Navy briefing on the CVN-78 program to CRS and CBO.

[11] Source: Transcript of hearing.

[12] Government Accountability Office, *Defense Acquisitions[:] Assessments of Selected Weapon Programs*, GAO-11-233SP, March 2011, p. 55.

[13] Department of Defense, *Selected Acquisition Report (SAR), CVN-78*, As of June 30, 2010, p. 7.
[14] Congressional Budget Office, *An Analysis of the Navy's Fiscal Year 2011 Shipbuilding Plan*, May 2010, pp. 11-13.
[15] Director, Operational Test and Evaluation, *FY 2010 Annual Report*, December 2010, p. 112.
[16] The funding tables were posted at
http://rules
[17] Source: Statement of Secretary of Defense Robert Gates, at April 6, 2009, news conference on his recommendations for the FY2010 defense budget.
[18] Northrop Grumman Shipbuilding statement dated May 1, 2009, entitled "NGSB Statement Regarding Extending the Time Interval between New Build Starts For the Ford Class of Aircraft Carriers," provided to CRS by Northrop Grumman.
[19] Government Accountability Office, *Defense Acquisitions[:] Assessments of Selected Weapon Programs*, GAO-10-388SP, March 2010, p. 54.
[20] This is the date of the cover letters to the congressional recipients. The report itself has a cover date of February 2010.
[21] Department of the Navy, *Report to Congress on Effects of Five-year Build Intervals for Force Class Aircraft Carriers*, February 2010, 5 pp. Copy provided to CRS by Navy Office of legislative Affairs on April 8, 2010.
[22] Department of Defense, *Selected Acquisition Report (SAR), CVN-78*, As of June 30, 2010, p. 26.
[23] Department of Defense, *Selected Acquisition Report (SAR), CVN-78*, As of December 31, 2009, pp. 4 and 25.
[24] Department of the Navy, *Report to Congress on Effects of Five-year Build Intervals for Force Class Aircraft Carriers*, February 2010, 5 pp. The cover letters sent with the report are dated March 4, 2010. Copy of report provided to CRS by Navy Office of legislative Affairs on April 8, 2010.

CHAPTER SOURCES

Chapter 1 - This is an edited, reformatted and augmented version of a Congressional Research Service publication, RL33946, dated January 18, 2011.

Chapter 2 - This is an edited, reformatted and augmented version of United States, Congressional Budget Office publication, dated May 2011.

Chapter 3 - This is an edited, reformatted and augmented version of a Congressional Research Service publication, RS20643, dated April 12, 2011.

INDEX

A

access, 15, 16, 21, 27, 60
adjustment, 63, 65
adverse effects, 22
agencies, 65
annual rate, 41, 49, 52, 58, 66, 69, 79
appropriations, 31, 38
Appropriations Act, 86
arithmetic, 56
assault, 10, 25, 26, 27, 29, 36, 40, 41, 42, 43, 44, 46, 48, 49, 50, 52, 54, 66, 68, 69
assessment, 32, 33, 83, 91, 94
assets, 72
attachment, 93
authority, 98

B

background information, 74
barriers, 4
base, 19, 20, 28, 30, 32, 38, 71, 75, 83, 90, 91, 94, 95, 97
benefits, 24, 59, 71, 88
Boat, 9, 18, 56, 89
bonds, 64, 65, 72
break-even, 10, 11, 12, 14, 15, 36, 52, 58, 69
burn, 3
business cycle, 63, 64
businesses, 60

C

candidates, 40, 42
cash, 46, 53, 59, 64
cash flow, 46, 59, 64
certification, 56, 71
challenges, 22, 26, 83, 85
China, 3
classes, 12, 20, 25, 26, 27, 29, 30, 42, 44, 49, 54, 59
climate, 57
combustion, 21
commercial, 3, 16, 26, 35, 37, 49, 56, 60
commodity, 55
compensation, 46, 60, 65
competition, 94
complement, 59
complexity, 20
computing, 63, 65
conference, 7, 26, 28, 31, 33, 78, 79, 90, 98, 99
configuration, 44
Congressional Budget Office, v, 36, 39, 40, 43, 45, 48, 52, 60, 64, 68, 69, 70, 71, 72, 79, 98, 99
construction, 6, 12, 17, 18, 19, 26, 28, 30, 31, 33, 38, 44, 54, 55, 56, 63,

65, 71, 75, 82, 83, 84, 87, 89, 90, 91, 94, 95, 96, 97, 98
consumers, 60
consumption, 42, 57
contingency, 2, 12, 15
cooling, 44, 55, 70, 85
coordination, 33
correlation, 64, 91, 96
cost-benefit analysis, 91
crises, 15
crude oil, 2, 10, 11, 12, 34, 36, 41, 58, 60

D

deflator, 36, 93
Department of Defense, 24, 25, 31, 37, 58, 74, 80, 86, 87, 92, 99
Department of Energy, 5, 60
diesel fuel, 36
displacement, 8, 9, 11, 25, 26, 27, 29, 32, 37, 46, 48, 53, 55, 57, 59, 68, 70
distribution, 20, 25, 40
DOT, 74, 80, 85
draft, 83

E

economic competitiveness, 8
economic resources, 63
electricity, 57
electromagnetic, 24, 80, 84
electronic systems, 50
emergency, 17
employment, 17
employment levels, 17
endurance, 30, 31
energy, 8, 11, 15, 30, 42, 50, 51, 70
engineering, 5, 18, 22, 30, 54, 84
environment, 14, 22, 82
environmental impact, 12, 21
equipment, 3, 16, 18, 35, 44, 82, 84, 90
Europe, 44

evidence, 28
executive branch, 65
Executive Order, 5
expenditures, 40, 48, 52, 53, 54, 55, 58, 68, 69
expertise, 19, 94

F

fabrication, 90
federal government, 59, 63
financial, 65
fiscal year 2009, 28, 32
fixed costs, 89
fixed rate, 66
flank, 24
flight, 42, 43, 48, 52, 55, 68, 69, 85
fluctuations, 60
food, 5, 51, 57
force, 5, 14, 15, 16, 22, 24, 27, 74, 75, 81, 87, 89, 97
Ford, v, viii, 8, 9, 13, 20, 35, 48, 54, 68, 70, 73, 74, 75, 79, 87, 89, 90, 92, 94, 95, 97, 98, 99
forecasting, 60
forward presence, 24
France, 3, 37
fuel consumption, 50, 57
funding, viii, 14, 22, 28, 53, 54, 73, 74, 75, 76, 77, 83, 84, 85, 86, 87, 88, 89, 94, 97, 98, 99
funds, 22, 32, 53, 86

G

GAO, 82, 90, 98, 99
Germany, 35
global demand, 60
goods and services, 71
greenhouse, 21
greenhouse gases, 21
gross domestic product, 54
growth, 25, 41, 50, 54, 58, 59, 60, 65, 66, 70, 74, 79, 80, 82, 84, 90, 98

growth rate, 42, 50, 66
guidance, 31

H

health, 59
historical data, 57, 59, 64
homes, 16
House, vii, 1, 2, 7, 10, 14, 22, 23, 26, 27, 29, 30, 31, 35, 36, 37, 39, 80, 86, 88, 98
House of Representatives, 98
housing, 59
housing benefit, 59
Hunter, 25
hybrid, 50

I

improvements, 75
income, 71
income tax, 71
India, 3
individuals, 91, 94, 95
industry, 19, 54, 60, 63
inflation, 41, 52, 54, 60, 65, 66, 69, 79, 84, 88, 91, 95, 96, 97
information technology, 85
infrastructure, 16, 20, 21, 25, 33, 57
integration, 17, 18, 85
interest rates, 72
Intervals, 88, 93, 94, 99
investment, 18, 20, 32, 72
investments, 46, 64, 65
investors, 46, 60, 64, 65
issues, vii, 12, 24, 25, 74, 79, 80, 98

J

Japan, 35

K

knots, 4

L

lasers, 24
lead, 31, 34, 49, 55, 82, 83, 84, 98
learning, 54, 79, 81, 83, 88, 89, 91, 95
legislation, 33, 38
LIFE, 34
lifetime, 12, 15, 41
light, 18, 25, 26, 27, 29, 37, 60
logistics, 24, 46, 57
LSD, 27, 29, 40, 41, 42, 44, 46, 47, 48, 49, 50, 52, 54, 55, 57, 58, 66, 67, 68, 69, 70, 71

M

machinery, 16
majority, 95
management, 71, 80
Marine Corps, 71
materials, 54
matter, iv
metals, 26
methodology, 34, 72
military, 3, 16, 35, 58, 71, 87
mission, 21, 30, 58
missions, 3, 5, 15, 44, 70
models, 53
modifications, 33, 34
modules, 19, 56
motor control, 82

N

National Defense Authorization Act, 23, 24, 25, 26, 27, 28, 29, 30, 32, 71, 94
natural disaster, 16
negative consequences, 83

next generation, 23, 30, 31, 32
North America, 60
Northeast Asia, 44
nuclear surface, 30
nuclear weapons, 3

O

Office of Management and Budget, 72
officials, 35, 37, 70, 82, 83, 84
oil, 10, 14, 21, 36, 40, 41, 42, 46, 49, 50, 51, 52, 55, 58, 60, 64, 65, 66, 69, 70, 71, 72
oil production, 60
operating costs, 53, 56, 63, 65
operations, 3, 4, 5, 8, 15, 16, 18, 24, 27, 31, 35, 39, 40, 42, 44, 48, 50, 52, 53, 68, 69, 70
opportunities, 2, 3, 9, 12
overhead costs, 79, 88, 90
oversight, 74, 80, 89

P

parallel, 33
Persian Gulf, 4
personal communication, 70
personnel costs, 49, 59
PET, 60
petroleum, vii, 3, 6, 21, 39, 40, 41, 42, 50, 57, 60
Petroleum, 60
plants, 13, 51, 56
platform, 95
policy, 26, 29, 36, 38
pollutants, 21
positive relationship, 63
POWER, 30
power generation, 26, 30
power plants, 5, 22, 51
preparation, iv
present value, 46, 51, 53, 59, 63, 64, 65, 70

President, 30, 33, 36, 38, 74, 75, 76, 84, 88, 97
presidential veto, 29
price index, 54
private firms, 63
probability, 84
producers, 60
project, 46, 53, 65
proliferation, 24, 25
protection, 30, 85

Q

quality assurance, 18

R

radar, 8, 15, 28, 44, 51, 58, 70, 82, 83
radiation, 26
radioactive waste, 21
ramp, 81, 95
rate of return, 64
recommendations, iv, 34, 74, 76, 78, 88, 98, 99
Reform, 25
reliability, 82, 85
repair, 12, 20, 57
reputation, 5, 21
requirements, 24, 25, 26, 28, 33, 80, 85, 89, 97
reserves, 60
resources, 32, 63
response, 11, 33, 71
restructuring, 82
retirement, 6, 8, 10, 59
retirement age, 8
risk, 28, 33, 46, 50, 53, 59, 63, 64, 65, 66, 72, 74, 76, 79, 81, 82, 95
risk assessment, 28
risks, 60, 83
rules, 99
Russia, 3

S

safety, 5, 22, 24, 25
savings, vii, viii, 14, 40, 41, 42, 51, 63, 65
Secretary of Defense, vii, 1, 2, 7, 24, 25, 26, 27, 28, 29, 30, 38, 74, 76, 78, 87, 88, 89, 91, 94, 98, 99
securities, 63
security, 24, 25
Senate, 7, 23, 25, 26, 28, 31, 86, 87, 88, 98
sensitivity, 42, 50, 60
sensors, 16, 24, 25
sequencing, 90
shape, 81
shock, 22
shortage, 60
short-term interest rate, 72
signs, 98
Singapore, 4
skimming, 85
software, 81, 82, 85
Soviet Union, 35
specifications, 43
spin, 75
stability, 60
state, 14, 97
states, 13, 14, 21, 28, 29, 33, 35, 36, 75, 83, 84, 87, 89, 91, 92
statistics, 56
steel, 63
storage, 25, 26
stress, 81
structure, 97
submarines, vii, 5, 9, 10, 14, 19, 21, 27, 29, 30, 31, 35, 36, 40, 44, 54, 56, 57, 70, 71, 89, 90, 92, 95
supervision, 39
supplier, 83, 88, 90, 94, 97
suppliers, 75, 83, 90, 94, 95, 96
support services, 64
surging, 15
surplus, 60
surveillance, 98

T

Taiwan, 4
target, 85, 98
taxes, 59
taxpayers, 60, 72
technical comments, 83
technical support, 94, 96
techniques, 34
technologies, 55, 80, 82, 84
technology, 22, 23, 26, 28, 34, 55, 83
temperature, 16, 35
tempo, 11, 12, 14, 15, 24
tension, 37
testing, 18, 19, 53, 80, 81, 82, 83, 85
thorium, 22, 24, 26
threats, 44
Title V, 33, 38
trade, 90, 91, 95, 97
training, 12, 20, 21, 33, 37, 90, 91, 95, 97
trajectory, 41, 42, 46, 49, 50, 58, 60, 65
transactions, 60
transmission, 16
transport, 27, 44, 60
transportation, 60
Treasury, 63, 64, 65, 67, 69, 72

U

U.S. policy, vii, 1, 2, 7, 29, 38
unit cost, 54, 83, 97
United, v, 3, 29, 30, 38, 39, 60, 87
United Kingdom, 3
United States, v, 3, 29, 30, 38, 39, 60, 87
up-front costs, vii, viii, 40
uranium, 21, 24, 35, 42

V

variations, 46
vehicles, 60
vessels, 22, 26, 27, 29, 30, 31, 32, 34, 38, 55, 56, 71, 87

volatility, 41
vulnerability, 16

W

waiver, 75
waste, 24, 25
waste disposal, 24

water, 21, 22, 35, 37
weapons, 3, 5, 24, 25
West Bank, 36
workers, 56
workforce, 18
workload, 56, 91, 95, 96, 97
worldwide, 21, 60